A Retrospective on Enabling a Connected World

The Race for the Original Primordial Soup

Shaun D'Souza

To my late father

Contents

Möbius strip

A RETROSPECTIVE ON ENABLING A CONNECTED WORLD

Prologue

The human mind has an innate ability to reason about its surrounding environment. Artificial Intelligence has grown in leaps and bounds from the punch card and calculator to the laptop and modern generation mobile software. This book is a compendium of my Machine Learning and Artificial Intelligence learnings. It contains a collection of Software and AI/ML manuscripts.

As academia and industry, we have vested interests in dissemination of software in society. We explore a broader ecosystems enabling for industry and academia confluence. We explore the AI journey as a contemporary technology. We look at the nuances of how we as a society perceive technology.

- Intelligent machines, Turing test, Web N, 10 Billion users

- Law of accelerating returns

AI is the ability to exhibit intelligent behaviour equivalent to or indistinguishable from a human. It presents an economic value in excess of 100 Trillion of market value. It hails the fourth industrial revolution since steam and the railroads. The fallout of these revolution is the creation of a socioeconomic middle class of >1 billion.

As was seen with the railroads, varying gauge sizes were used to exclude competition. Standardization brought about wider adoption of the railroads through policy regulation causality. The underlying philosophy of the book stems from the culinary inspiration of that "If Yan can cook, so can you!".

It is conventionally believed in some circles that intelligent alien lifeforms would have made contact with life on earth in its beginning. Early algorithms in Search used rule-based approaches. These rules had to be explicitly defined and were difficult to maintain, more so in a transient employee organization. In a transient jobs market these presented challenges including finding and updating a rule in a legacy design. Recent approaches to search such as Bing on the other hand have used Machine Learning based approaches where rules do not have to be explicitly defined.

Bill Gates has said that a breakthrough in Machine Learning would be worth 10 Microsoft's. Today we see this more so with companies like Uber. These bridge a key socio-economic gap. There is a gap in the markets and capitalizations in the developing world. These economies have been founded in consumer centric mindsets. It is an imperative that these become producer centric bridging a large imbalance in the 21st century. It will be an overarching theme to subsidize the tail end of this conversation. Software and Business are 2 sides of the same coin and must co-exist to foster community. In doing so however I do not wish to take you to refrigerator school but rather broadly outline the current state of the affairs and challenges in the enterprise.

I present a laundry list of items that I'd imagined would find place in a consolidated book edition. The tree and maze illustrate a dichotomy in software and systems infrastructure. They are essential ingredients in an ecosystem. Use cases include the rationalization of taxonomies/thesauri and cognitive biases. Eg. man-woman, snakes-ladders, import-export, left-right, train-test.

Brain in a vat

A RETROSPECTIVE ON ENABLING A CONNECTED WORLD

Chapter 1

LSTM Neural Network for Textual Ngrams

Cognitive neuroscience is the study of how the human brain functions on tasks like decision making, language, perception and reasoning. Deep learning is a class of machine learning algorithms that use neural networks. They are designed to model the responses of neurons in the human brain. Learning can be supervised or unsupervised. Ngram token models are used extensively in language prediction. Ngrams are probabilistic models that are used in predicting the next word or token. They are a statistical model of word sequences or tokens and are called Language Models or Lms. Ngrams are essential in creating language prediction models. We are exploring a broader sandbox ecosystems enabling for AI. Specifically, around Deep learning applications on unstructured content form on the web.

1.1 Ngrams

Ngram models work on the basis that we can predict the next token given the previous n-1 tokens. We use the following notation to compute the probability of a word sequence. In order to represent a random variable X taking on the value y we use $P(X = "y")$ or the simplification $P(y)$. Now, to compute the joint probability of a sequence of words $w_1...w_n$ we use $P(w_1, w_2, ..., w_n)$.

We compute the probability of an entire sequence of word by decomposing this probability using the chain rule of probability

$$P(w_1, w_2, ..., w_n) = P(w_1|w_2, ..., w_n) * P(w_2|w_3, ..., w_n)$$
$$* P(w_3|w_4, ..., w_n) * P(w_n)$$

The chain rule shows the relation between computing the joint probability of a sequence of words given the conditional probability of the previous sequence of words. Using a Ngram model allows us to further simplify this equation as we estimate the probability of a word given its history by approximating the last N words. A Bigram model for example would use the conditional probability of a word given the word before it.

$$P(w_1|w_2, ..., w_n) \approx P(w_1|w_2) = \frac{C(w_1, w_2)}{C(w_2)} \quad (1.1)$$

A trigram model allows us to improve our predictability by using the preceding 2 word tokens.

$$P(w_1|w_2, ..., w_n) \approx P(w_1|w_2, w_3) * P(w_2|w_3) \quad (1.2)$$

The easiest way to estimate these probabilities is using the count value of the token sequences in the training data.

$$P(w_1|w_2, ..., w_n) = \frac{C(w_1, w_2, ..., w_n)}{C(w_2, ..., w_n)} \quad (1.3)$$

To obtain the count values for our tokens we use the ngram utility Michel et al. [2010] to obtain a set of token sequence counts for all the data in the training set. For the purposes of our investigation we used the textual book data from the Gutenberg project and Brown data set. The Google Books Ngram Corpus Lin et al. [2012] is available at http://books.google.com/ngrams.

Total 9624 unique ngrams in 890415 1-grams	
the	50869
N	32481
of	24406
to	23662
a	21639

Table 1.1: 1-grams

1.2   Entropy and perplexity

We process the data to obtain the 5-gram tokens using the ngram utility which gives us a count value of
all consequent tokens in the training data. We are using textual data for the purposes of our investigation
on computing the ngram probabilities.

We use a variety of smoothing techniques to nor-
malize the data and since a large number of token sequences are not in the training data. We use a ngram
log probability (NGLP) to estimate the probability
of our language model. This allows us to maintain
a sum value of the log probability for the training
data as it is difficult to compute accumulated prod-

Total 273906 unique ngrams in 890414 2-grams	
N_N	7204
of_the	5293
in_the	4507
N_million	4493
to_N	2865

Table 1.2: 2-grams

Total 613476 unique ngrams in 890413 3-grams	
the_u_s	920
N_million_or	687
of_N_million	665
N_a_share	631
million_or_N	621

Table 1.3: 3-grams

3-grams	entropy	7.95
	perplexity	247

Table 1.4: Cross entropy

uct value on decimal values. We use these values to compute the cross entropy of the data.

$$Crossentropy = H = -(log2(P(w_1|w_2, w_3)$$
$$+ log2(P(w_2|w_3, w_4)) + ...log2(P(w_n - 2|w_n - 1, w_n))$$

This allows us to compute the cross entropy of the data on the test set which gives us a measure of how well our language model is able to predict the tokens in the code. We calculate a perplexity value equivalent to 2^H.

A low cross entropy means that we are able to accurately predict the next token. If the model predicts every token correctly with a probability of 1, then our cross entropy is 0. We use this data to study multiple types of identifiers in the code including variable and class field definitions, method names and function calls in the code.

Figure 1.1: Zipf distribution

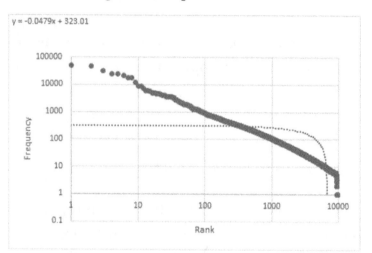

We measured the zipf distribution - Fig. 1.1 of the data in the text Allamanis and Sutton [2013]. As per Zipf's law we see that the frequency of the tokens in the data set is inversely proportional to its rank in the number count of tokens. The training data contained 9624 unique tokens. The slope is -0.0479.

We plan to extend this code to deep learning applications on unstructured content form on the web along the lines of the Google Brain project Abadi et al. [2016] and TensorFlow Abadi et al. [2015]. This will allow us to build a knowledge base Rastogi [2012] using existing projects and reuse code as per the application.

1.3 Neural network language models

TensorFlow is an open source library for deep learning developed by Google. It is a python library that is similar to numpy, scipy and uses data flow graphs and tensors for numerical computation. They support the development of neural networks using a set of libraries. A perceptron is a simple neural network designed to use a threshold activation function. It computes the activation of a neuron using the dot product of the input and weight vectors.

$$O(x) = sgn(\sum_{i=0}^{n} w_i * x_i) \qquad (1.4)$$

$$\text{where } sgn(y) = \begin{cases} 1 & \text{if } y > 0 \\ -1 & \text{otherwise.} \end{cases}$$

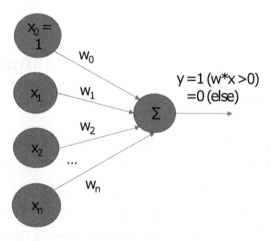

Figure 1.2: Single layer perceptron

Fig. 1.2 shows a single layer perceptron. For a given dataset the perceptron is guaranteed to find a linear plane of separation described as the hyperplane decision surface in the n-dimension space. The perceptron training rule is used iteratively to update the network weights. The weight vectors are initialized randomly and updated using the rule

$$w_i \leftarrow w_i + \Delta w_i$$
$$\Delta w_i = \eta(t - o)x \qquad (1.5)$$

Additionally, multiple layers can be used in a multi-layer perceptron. This is effective on uni-dimensional data and finds application in a number of natural language processing tasks Carreras and Màrquez [2005], Metzler and Kurland [2012] including part of speech (POS) tagging. The OpenNLP library uses a multi-layer perceptron in its trained model. These have been effectively used in applications in information extraction as shown in Chapter 2. D'souza [2018] demonstrated the use of a chunker model in detection of semantic triples.

A neural network uses a continuous activation function in each of the layers. Some of the activation functions are in Table 1.5.

Fig. 1.3 shows an artificial neural network with

Sigmoid	Softmax	Hyperbolic tangent
$\sigma(y) =$ $\dfrac{1}{1+e^{-y}}$	$f(x) =$ $\dfrac{e^x}{\sum_{j=1}^{N} e^{x_j}}$	$tanh(x) =$ $\dfrac{1 - e^{-2x}}{1 + e^{-2x}}$

Table 1.5: Activation functions

Figure 1.3: Neural Network.

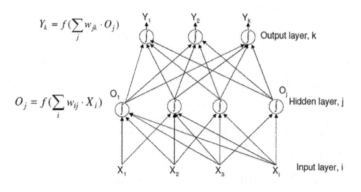

Sigmoid activations. The weights in the hidden layer are used in determination of word vectors used in the Continuous Bag-of-words (CBOW) and Skip-gram models Mikolov et al. [2013]. These are used in predicting semantic similarity. We use a

CHAPTER 1. LSTM NEURAL NETWORK FOR TEXTUAL NGRAMS

TensorFlow Keras LSTM layer - Fig. 1.4 to output word sentences in the PTB corpus. Below is a generated text sequence corresponding to an input seed value. This can be used in applications like the Google Smart compose for autocompletion of input text given a suitable corpus of training data.

```
----- Generating with seed: "n plant near <unk>
    ill. was completed in n <eos> in a disputed n
     ruling the commerce commission said
    commonwealth edison could raise its
    electricity rates by $ n million to pay for
    the plant <eos> but state courts upheld"
```

```
n plant near <unk> ill. was completed in n <eos>
     in a disputed n ruling the commerce
    commission said commonwealth edison could
    raise its electricity rates by $ n million to
     pay for the plant <eos> but state courts
    upheld a challenge of last year 's that list
    of the low 's action action of the low are to
     debt higher prices the in financing <eos>
    the u.s. until that the latest will leave <
```

```
eos> the and and japan is expected to slip <
eos> the funds have money funds have received
 these rich since that the decline plot
increase <unk> with the low and japan
automobile said that the u.s. is that that u.
s. is is already for a request <eos> the
decline and japan of their program managers
the highest has authority dropped n n in
september <eos> first n n for export and $ n
million debt and year plant <eos>
```

1.4   Summary

We explore the use of the TensorFlow library in creating a recurrent neural network (RNN). We train a
LSTM neural network on textual data from the Penn
Tree bank corpus. We see that the LSTM is able to
accurately predict the word ngrams using a seed sentence. We plan to extend the work to use POS and
chunker sequences Honnibal and Johnson [2015] in
phrase construction. We continue to explore the in-
tersection of Software and Business in the context of

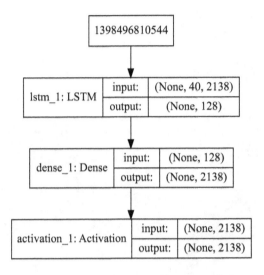

Figure 1.4: Keras LSTM model

AI, Globalization, CSR and the Last mile with an emphasis on Deep learning applications in the broader web.

Demography of a 7 billion

Chapter 2

Parser Extraction of Triples in Unstructured Text

The web contains vast repositories of unstructured text. We investigate the opportunity for building a knowledge graph from these text sources. We generate a set of triples which can be used in knowledge gathering and integration. We define the architecture of a language compiler for processing subject-predicate-object triples using the OpenNLP parser. We implement a depth-first search traversal on the POS tagged syntactic tree appending predicate and object information. A parser enables higher precision and higher recall extractions of syntactic relationships across conjunction boundaries. We are able to extract 2-2.5 times the correct extractions of ReVerb. The extractions are used in a variety of semantic web applications and question answering. We verify extraction of 50,000 triples on the ClueWeb dataset.

2.1 Context-free grammars

There is a considerable amount of research in natural language processing (NLP). With the availability of a larger set of NLP tools like OpenNLP OpenNLP [2011], it is today possible to POS tag and chunk vast amount of unstructured text that is available on the internet. Projects like ClueWeb, OpenIE and Wikipedia provide a corpus of text data which can be used for ontological engineering. OpenNLP supports the POS tagging and chunking of data. It outputs a parse tree for the data which encapsulates the syntactic content in a n-ary tree data structure. POS tag data provides a higher level of understanding as compared to a bag of words approach to web search today. We explore opportunities for language inference and understanding through subject-predicate-object analysis of web scale unstructured data.

Various methods are used to extract subject-predicate-object triples in unstructured data. DBpedia extractor is used to generate triples using annotated field information in Wikipedia. OpenIE Etzioni et al. [2011] used POS and chunker data while ClauseIE Del Corro and Gemulla [2013] uses a parser to output a set of word triples.

Bootstrapping functions use N-gram models to generate a template for a given combination of noun phrases. These are used to search a larger corpus of data for similar templates and generate values. NER taggers are used to annotate person and location information. We assume a context free grammar (CFG) for English language Hopcroft et al. [2001].

$$G \;=\; (N, \Sigma, R, S)$$

$$N \;\in\; \{non-terminal\ symbols\}$$
$$\Sigma \;\in\; \{terminal\ symbols\}$$
$$R \;\in\; \{rules\}\ of\ the\ form\ X \to Y_1 Y_n$$
$$for\ n \geq 0, X \in N, Y_i \in (N \cup \Sigma)$$
$$S \;\in\; N\ start\ symbol\ \{TOP\}$$

$$N \;=\; \{S, NP, VP, PP, DT, VB, NN, IN\}$$
$$S \;=\; S$$
$$\Sigma \;=\; word\ in\ the\ English\ language$$

$$
\begin{aligned}
R \;=\; & S \to NP\,VP \\
& VP \to VB \\
& VP \to VB\,NP \\
& VP \to VP\,PP \\
& NP \to DT\,NN \\
& NP \to NP\,PP \\
& PP \to IN\,NP
\end{aligned}
$$

2.2 N-ary parser

We found a limitation of extractors that were unable to extract the verb phrase accurately and instead appended a large amount of additional words including the trailing noun and preposition context. The extractors were unable to process sentence and conjunction values resulting in incorrect verb and object phrases. A parse tree is able to capture conjunction and object phrase information correctly. Although there is an overhead on the parsing time.

We evaluate the parser tree for sequences of NP noun phrases (subject, object) and VB - verbs (predicate). OpenNLP generates a parse tree using the CFG rules. We implement an in-order traversal of the syntactic tree to detect SVO phrases. We maintain a list of all NP phrases in the sentence. We then traverse the tree to detect subject object pairs and the predicate.

Algorithm 1 Subject-predicate phrase algorithm

---

function SUBJECT-NOUN-PHRASE(*parse*)
    kids ← *CHILD*(*parse*)
    for i = 1 to SIZE(kids) **do**
        if TYPE(kids[i]) = NP **then**
            subject = kids[i]
            for j = i + 1 to SIZE(kids) **do**
                if TYPE(kids[j]) = VP **or** PP **or** SBAR **then**
                    explored ← an empty set

```
            while kids[j] not in explored do
                extraction ← APPEND(subject,
PREDICATE-VERB-PHRASE(kids[j]))
                    PRINT(extraction)
            end while
        end if
      end for
    end if
    SUBJECT-NOUN-PHRASE(kids[i])
  end for
end function


function PREDICATE-VERB-PHRASE(parse) re-
turn solution, failure
    kids ← CHILD(parse)
    initialize predicate string to be empty
    for i = 1 to SIZE(kids) do
        if TYPE(kids[i]) = VP or S then
            if kids[i] not in explored then
                return APPEND(predicate,
PREDICATE-VERB-PHRASE(kids[i]))
            end if
```

else if TYPE(kids[i]) = VB **or** JJ **or** RB **or** MD **or** TO **or** ADVP **or** DT **or** NN **or** IN **then**

$predicate \leftarrow APPEND(predicate, kids[i])$

for j = i + 1 to SIZE(kids) **do**

if TYPE(kids[j]) = NP **or** PP **or** ADJP **or** S **or** SBAR **then**

return APPEND(predicate, OBJECT-NOUN-PHRASE(kids[j]))

end if

end for

end if

end for

add parse to explored

return failure

end function

Algorithm 2 Object phrase algorithm

---

function OBJECT-NOUN-PHRASE($parse$) **return** solution, failure

$found \leftarrow false$

$kids \leftarrow CHILD(parse)$

initialize object string to be empty

for i = 1 to SIZE(kids) **do**

    if TYPE(kids[i]) = NP **or** S **then**

        $found \leftarrow true$

        if kids[i] not in explored **then**

            return APPEND(object, OBJECT-NOUN-PHRASE(kids[i]))

        else

            return APPEND(object, GET-COVERED-TEXT(kids[i]))

        end if

    else if TYPE(kids[i]) = PP **then**

        if kids[i] not in explored **then**

        return APPEND(object, OBJECT-PREPOSTION-PHRASE(kids[i]))

        else

            return APPEND(object, GET-COVERED-TEXT(kids[i]))

        end if

    else if TYPE(kids[i]) = IN **or** TO **then**

        $object \leftarrow APPEND(object, kids[i])$

```
        end if
    end for
    add parse to explored
    if not found and TYPE(parse) = NP then
        return APPEND(object, parse)
    end if
    return failure
end function


function OBJECT-PREPOSITION-PHRASE(parse)
return solution, failure
    kids ← CHILD(parse)
    initialize preposition string to be empty
    for i = 1 to SIZE(kids) do
        if TYPE(kids[i]) = NP and not in explored
then
            return APPEND(preposition,
OBJECT-NOUN-PHRASE(kids[i]))
        else if TYPE(kids[i]) = PP and not in ex-
plored then
            return APPEND(preposition,
OBJECT-PREPOSTION-PHRASE(kids[i]))
```

else if TYPE(kids[i]) $=$ IN **or** TO **or** JJ **or** ADVP **then**

$$preposition \leftarrow APPEND(preposition, kids[i])$$

    end if

    end for

    add parse to explored

    return failure

end function

We implement a depth-first search on the n-ary parse tree. We search the parse tree for a noun-verb phrase indicating the subject-predicate - Fig. 1. The noun phrase is used as the subject in the clause. We look for a verb phrase VP or preposition phrase PP in the siblings. In the case of subsequent conjunctions CC and WHNP phrases, we continue to search the sibling nodes. For all found VP, PP we search for the predicate clause in the sentence. A predicate clause consists of a sequence of verb, adjectives, adverb and modal identifiers. These are appended to a string of predicates. VP phrases are searched recursively till we find a terminal NP object clause. We represent the SVO in the triples format. We use a training set of 200 phrases from earlier publications on information extraction. These give us a range of parse trees to evaluate the search on and refine.

Earlier work on information extraction was limited to the capabilities of the POS and Chunker tags. Verb phrases were detected using statistical probabilities of frequently occurring patterns in the English language. We implement a rigorous parse tree design which preserves the language syntax of the text data.

As there is a high availability of computing today in the cloud, we implement the SVO parser as an offline function to process the syntactic tree. We parse all the sentences in the text and generate a parsed output. This is subsequently used to generate the SVO triples. With the availability of computing we can improve performance of the parser by parallelizing the parsing of input sentences.

We contrast the SVO triples with past research including OpenIE and ClauseIE. We find that a parser based approach is able to extract a large number of SVO's accurately. Availability of a syntactic parse tree also enables us to extract triples with reduced ambiguity. The obtained triples map exactly to sub-trees in the sentence parse tree and capture all the semantic information - subject predicate. The n-ary parse tree encapsulates the syntactic structure of the sentence completely.

We are able to precisely extract SVO information. In the initial revision of the code we implemented predicate extractions to include the trailing noun phrase. This was updated to resolve the object clause to contain the noun phrase NP and a trailing preposition phrase PP - Fig. 2. We use a set of heuristics to maximize the number of triples generated for each noun phrase, verb phrase.

2.3   Triples extraction

The SVO extractions are coherent as OpenNLP captures the language syntax in the parse tree. We compare the number of extractions with the ReVerb extractor. We observe a larger number of triples as we are searching for all noun phrases in the object. The NLP parser is able to extract a large number of triples matching ReVerb and ClausIE.

Example sentence

The principal opposition parties boycotted the polls after accusations of vote rigging, and the only other name on the ballot was a little known challenger from a marginal political party

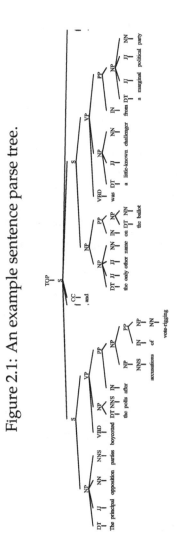

Figure 2.1: An example sentence parse tree.

("The principal opposition parties", "boycotted",
"the polls")

("The principal opposition parties", "boycotted",
"the polls after accusations")

("The principal opposition parties", "boycotted",
"the polls after accusations of vote rigging")

("the only other name on the ballot", "was", "a little
known challenger")

("the only other name on the ballot", "was", "a little
known challenger from a marginal political party")

The above extractions are labelled correctly in
the ReVerb dataset and contain some redundant
extractions. We evaluated the parser extraction on
the ClueWeb12 dataset and were able to extract more
than 50,000 triples. We found that the parser was
able to perform on par with ReVerb and ClausIE.
This was achieved using the syntactic functionality
in the parse tree - Fig. 2.1. It demonstrates the ability
of a parser based approach in extracting high quality
triples.

We verified the extractions for a sample set of

sentences in the OpenIE and ClausIE publications. These were used to ensure precision in the parser extractions. We additionally ran the parser on the ClueWeb data and compared the number of extractions with the alternative approaches. We measured the distribution of the noun and verb sub-trees in the sentence text - Table 2.1. We found that 10% of the phrases were prepositional. The density of the noun and verb phrases are in agreement with the English context free grammar (CFG).

Earlier works like OpenIE and ReVerb have looked at the extraction of subject-verb-object (SVO) triples. They were however based primarily on the availability of POS and chunker data. Structure of the verb and noun phrases were determined using statistical distribution of the phrases in text data. ClausIE used a dependency parser in resolving the SVO relations.

Projects like DBpedia Auer et al. [2007] were designed to extract structured data in the information box and map it to an ontology. Tgrep2 Rohde [2001] enable us to extract and parse a tree without explic-

Table 2.1: Phrase distribution

Noun	Frequency
NP → NN	14%
NP → NP PP	12%
NP → DT NN	12%
NP → NN NN	6%

Verb	Frequency
VP → VB NP	16%
VP → VB VP	10%
VP → TO VP	9%
VP → VB PP	8%
VP → VB	6%

Preposition	Frequency
PP → IN NP	81%
PP → TO NP	9%

itly coding the rules. A set of regular expressions are used to extract matching sub-trees.

We evaluated a number of extractions on the ReVerb, Wikipedia and NYT dataset. We obtained the sample dataset from the ClausIE sources. We

Figure 2.2: Number of correct non-redundant extractions.

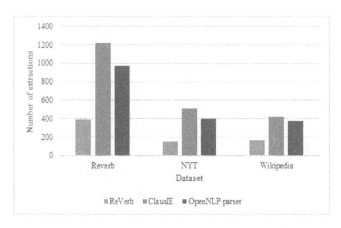

were able to extract more than 2000 SVO in the dataset with 1000 matching the ClausIE extractions.

As all the extracted results are semantically accurate, the precision of the results is 0.9. This value is independent of the dataset and is derived from the extraction grammar rules. The extractions are based on a rule based system and capture the syntax of the English language. Some of the SVO outputs are incorrect due to the ambiguities in the language parse tree including conjunctions in noun phrases. We ver-

	Precision	Recall
NYT	0.8	0.64
Wikipedia	0.8	0.71
ReVerb	0.8	0.53

Table 2.2: Precision and recall values for various datasets

ified the extracted triples to measure the recall of the data. The recall value is a function of the grammar. We can refine the rules to find additional triples in the data. This would increase the recall on the extracted values. We measured an average recall value of 60% on the triples - Table 2. We used the extractions-all-labeled as a baseline for our computation. These include all the extractions from ReVerb, ClausIE and other OIE utilities.

We estimated a precision of 0.8 for the parser extractions. We found that the parser was able to extract 2-2.5 times the correct extractions of ReVerb and 80% of the correct non-redundant ClausIE extractions - Fig. 2.2.

2.4   Summary

We presented a methodology for extraction of subject-predicate-object triples in a text corpus. We plan to extend this work to a larger ontological engineering for knowledge inference. We found that a syntactic parser was able to accurately extract triples in a text. We explored opportunities to further extend this work in translating an unstructured corpus of data into a semantic ontology. A user is able to explore the text using a triples structure.

Infrastructure hockey sticks. Technology easter egg, cliché #whatisinfrastructure #humanintheloop #humanoutoftheloop

Chapter 3

Evolving System Bottlenecks in the As A Service Cloud

The web ecosystem is rapidly evolving with changing business and functional models. Cloud platforms are available in a SaaS, PaaS and IaaS model designed around commoditized Linux based servers. 10 billion users will be online and accessing the web and its various content. The industry has seen a convergence around IP based technology. Additionally, Linux based designs allow for a system wide profiling of application characteristics. The customer is an OEM who provides Linux based servers for telecom solutions. The end customer will develop business applications on the server. Customers are interested in a latency profiling mechanism which helps them to understand how the application behaves at run time. The latency profiler is supposed to find the code path which makes an application block on I/O, and other synchronization primitives. This will allow the customer to understand the performance bottleneck and tune the system and application parameters.

3.1 Introduction

Web N. Open source has enabled the development of more efficient internet systems. As application performance is a top constraint, profiling is used to verify the performance of a multi-process and multi-threaded workloads. Additionally, a good developer always makes the optimal use of the platform architecture resources. Applications are deployed today in cloud environment and as a developer it is key to ensure that the code is well documented including maintenance of architectural UML diagrams to ensure minimal errors. Cloud computing combined with service-oriented architecture (SOA) and parallel computing have influenced application software development. Code is implemented in a variety of frameworks to ensure performance including OpenMP, MPI, MapReduce Dean and Ghemawat [2008] and Hadoop. Parallel programs present a variety of challenges including race conditions, synchronization and load balancing overhead.

Virtualization. This hosted infrastructure is complemented by a set of virtualization utilities that enable rapid provisioning and deployment of the web infrastructure in a distributed environment. Virtualization abstracts the underlying platform from the OS enabling a flexible infrastructure. Developers can partition resources across multiple running applications to ensure maximum utilization of resources. Additionally, systems can be ported across platforms with ease. Virtualization enables isolation of application run-time environment including kernel libraries ensuring that multi-threaded and multi-process workloads run in a scalable manner without errors. It decouples product development platforms from the conventional SDLC models enabling existing infrastructure to scale in available resources. The virtualization layer enables application profiling and development.

Open Source. Additionally, the cloud ecosystem is supported by the Open Source community enabling an accelerated scale of development and collaboration Mahmood and Saeed [2013]. This has been enabled by the internet and version control systems.

OOP and Java have enabled enterprise system architecture. Java is an algorithms, web and enterprise centric programming language. It allows for deployment of applications on a host of platforms running a virtual machine. 3 billion mobile devices run Java. Enterprise applications provide the business logic for an enterprise. Architectures have evolved from monolithic systems, to distributed tiered systems, to Internet connected cloud systems today.

Computing and the internet are more accessible and available to the larger community. Machine learning D'souza [2018] has made extensive advances with the availability of modern computing. It is used widely in Natural Language Processing, Speech Recognition and Web Search.

- Web N, 10 Billion users, Intelligent machines, Turing test

- Social media, enterprise mobility, data analytics and cloud

- Technology and enterprise

- Virtualization, Open Source

- Machine learning, compilers, algorithms, systems

3.2   Queries

We evaluate the customer application in the internet. We developed a full-system simulator to evaluate web workloads in a server client environment including network. We found opportunity for the use of virtualization technology to efficiently utilize cloud resources. Additionally, use the virtualization layers for performance related benchmarking functionality.

Review the use of profiling tools with the customer including COTS commercial solutions and alternative open source solutions. Both tools present a set of tradeoffs which would vary in the customer application. A commercial solution like Intel VTune, VMware vmkperf would be suitable for a range of applications and provide more accurate profiling data on a host platform running Windows.

However, as part of our solution implementation we will be reviewing the use of an open source solution in Linux perf and Xenoprof (OProfile). We would review the nature of the customer application including availability of source code. Additionally, we would assess the availability of a high level software architecture specification including UML, use case diagrams. These would allow us to evaluate a first-order survey of the system application bottlenecks on the target platform. This would include the choice of application UI (presentation layer), middle layer (business logic layer) and data access (data layer).

We would evaluate the application run time environment. If the application is implemented in C++ it would support the symbol tagged Linux kernel libraries. A java application would run with a compatible Java Runtime Environment (JRE) to ensure detection of class binary symbol information. We would evaluate the possibility of using the application source code vs. benchmarking the application binary. A binary would allow us to profile application performance information. Availability of source code would allow us to profile the application in a simulation environment including addition of custom flags and debug messages to benchmark the application. It would further allow us to customize the application to improve performance on the host platform.

As internet platforms evolve towards a cloud service model, we would evaluate the application runtime environment and opportunities for hosting the application in a private, public cloud. This would ensure application performance and scalability in a deployed setting. The application would scale in the usage model and number of users on a cloud platform.

Ensure customer is aligned with current business and technology environment. Architect and design cloud applications to support multitenancy, concurrency management, parallel processing and service-oriented architecture supporting rest services.

- Law of accelerating returns

- Prices and margins, competition, converging global supply and demand, evolving business models

- Tier vs. batch processing, open source (availability of source code), language – C++, Java, security and reliability.

- Public cloud - SaaS, PaaS, IaaS, in-house

- Numbers of users, usage model

- Structured data

- Web N, Availability of cloud computing platforms – SaaS, PaaS, IaaS. Use of virtualization infrastructure. Rapid provisioning and performance profiling of available resources

- Simulation. Full system simulation of end-end internet. Order of magnitude (slower)

- Type of application. Web based application hosted on a cloud computing platform.

3.3 Assumptions related to functionality / requirements

There is a host of cloud computing infrastructure deployed on Linux based platforms. Linux is open source and supports benchmarking and profiling of various applications. Additionally, it supports the use of Virtualization like Xen and VMware. We use OOP languages including Java, C++ and python. A NoSQL database MongoDB to store the profiling results data. This data is read and output to a web browser using Meteor web server. Kibana is used to store the profiling data in Elasticsearch. A dashboard is created to analyze the data in a user viewable histogram and pie chart.

- **Web N.** The internet is increasingly accessible to more than 10 billion users. It has been designed around Internet protocols and standards. The next generation of the web will use various Semantic web technologies.

- **Cloud computing.** Rapidly commoditized infrastructure and Linux servers

- Linux, Python, NoSQL Database MongoDB, Meteor web server, Kibana

- **Knowledge systems.** Vast repositories of structured, unstructured data

- **Efficient programming languages.** github

With the exponential growth in technology development in the recent years we find that developers have increased access to commoditized compute technology, Chapter 4. Platforms based on commodity Linux solution are widely deployed in the enterprise. Application developers are concerned about application performance and scalability in the cloud. Application performance bottlenecks are constantly evolving in a tiered internet. They vary around system constraints limitations in the kernel functionality. However, application scalability is bounded in fundamental constraints of application development arising from a producer consumer model. The Producer Consumer or Bounded buffer problem is an example of a multi-process synchronization challenge. It forms a central role in any Operating system design that allows concurrent process activity.

```
semaphore empty, mutex, full

function PRODUCER
    while (true) do
        WAIT(empty);
        WAIT(mutex);
        // add item
        // increment "head"
        SIGNAL(mutex);
        SIGNAL (full);

function CONSUMER
    while (true) do
        WAIT(full);
        WAIT(mutex);
        // remove item
```

```
// increment "tail"
SIGNAL(mutex);
SIGNAL(empty);
```

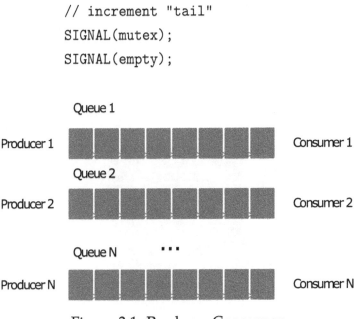

Figure 3.1: Producer Consumer

As we have N producers, N consumers and
N queues in the application – Fig. 3.1 we can see
that there are opportunities for the synchronization
through the use of semaphores, deadlock avoidance
and starvation. If we imagine infinite resources then
the producer continues writing to the queue and the
consumer has only to wait till there is data in the

queue. The dining philosopher's problem is another demonstration of the challenges in concurrency and synchronization.

3.3.1   Application workloads today

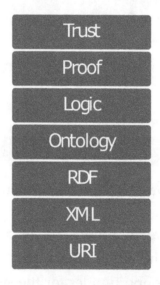

Figure 3.2: Semantic web stack

In the broader context of the internet it is always beneficial to host resources close to the client consumption including providing a larger bandwidth to the consumer. Additionally, open platforms and standards enable for a balanced distribution of available bandwidth resources allowing for a scalable platform for 10 billion consumers. Innovation and advancement is enabled through open source and open platforms around internet based wireless technology. The protocol stacks comprising the future semantic web data are as – Fig. 3.2.

3.4 Technical Risks & Mitigation plan

3.5 Modeling Notation

1. Unified Modeling Language (UML)

    (a) Class diagram

    (b) Use case

    (c) Sequence

2. Eclipse

Development environment	Availability of compilers and code generators. Availability of full-system Linux simulator supporting customer application functionality.
Technology	Custom application binary support for user profiling tools including symbol tag information. Generation of dependency graphs. Recompilation of driver libraries.
Availability of source code	Annotated source code. Proprietary system applications.
Customer application environment	Support for virtualization technology for Host OS and application compatibility.
Product size, Business impact, Customer related	Code reuse, Open source, Revenue, delivery deadline, New customer, customer reviews

Table 3.1: Top 5 Risk and mitigation

3. JDeveloper

4. JavaScript wavi

See Fig. 3.3.

3.6   Comparative Analysis

3.6.1   Alternative options considered

There are a wide range of profiling tools for the Linux
kernel.

1. Data collection

   (a) sysstat package – iostat, pidstat

   (b) sar, atop

2. Online data - top

   (a) iotop, iftop

3. Tracing – strace, perf_events, mutrace, ftrace

   (a) perf-tools, gprof

A RETROSPECTIVE ON ENABLING A CONNECTED WORLD

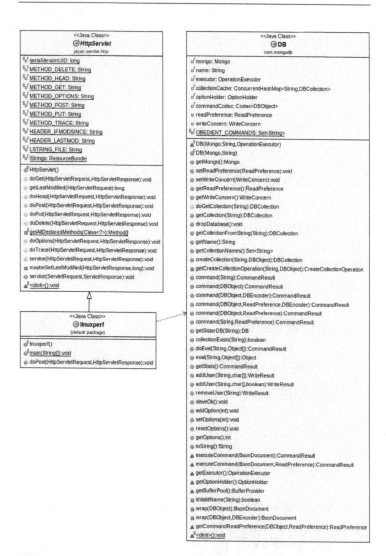

Figure 3.3: Tomcat MongoDB server

CHAPTER 3. EVOLVING SYSTEM BOTTLENECKS IN THE AS A SERVICE CLOUD

Virtualization technology is now common in the internet datacenter. It is also used for performance gathering. Will the customer be deploying the application in a private / public cloud? Evaluate the application in the cloud infrastructure. Increasingly vendors are adopting an as a service model for hosting applications on a platform. Evaluate opportunities for improving the application performance using native and hosted virtualization techniques. As per the type of application there are a host of performance profiling environments including perf, Intel VTune, VMware vmkperf.

System level application analysis is supported in Unix through the use of top, ps, vmstat, sar. However, these applications only allow for visibility and performance metrics at the application level. Additionally, Unix top allows the user to measure application compute and memory resource utilization. It provides information on processes running in the application.

Simulators are used to benchmark application systems. M5 Binkert et al. [2011] is a full-system simulator and supports modeling of compute, memory and network components. We implement an accurate view of the user system in a simulation environment. The simulator enables full system visibility of the technology stack allowing the user to configure application and kernel OS. Additionally, it is an open source simulator and can be extended to implement customer functionality to benchmark the application. It supports tracing of application and kernel function calls.

There are a host of cloud platforms available to deploy the customer application in a web environment. Cloud environment enables scalability of the application. As per the vendor environment there are a number of utilities to evaluate application performance in the cloud.

System bottlenecks are constantly evolving. As infrastructure is increasingly being commoditized with a growth of development around open source technologies. It is essential that adequate bandwidth is provisioned in the cloud to allow for application scalability. Virtualization technology enables efficient partitioning of additional resources. As a metric, it is key to replicate scale the infrastructure maintaining redundancy to ensure quality of service in the end-to-end internet.

At the same time, it is good to ensure efficient code is developed and maintained. There are a host of projects on github that allow for efficient development of user application code.

Additionally, availability of source code enables for maintenance of code counters to measure performance. We developed a full-system simulator M5. It enables application profiling in a simulation environment including server client.

The simulator is available as open source and allows you to model compute, memory and network functionality in the system. It is an event driven simulator and supports benchmarking of key workload characteristics, check pointing, forwarding and replay. Additionally, these capabilities can be extended in the simulator ecosystem including updation of the Linux kernel to support the application code functionality and profiling. The simulator and Linux environment are accessible online. However, as we are enabling the performance profiling in simulation we do have the disadvantage that metrics gathering is at 10X slower as the entire system is running in a simulation environment.

3.7   Recommended option

As a solution we would take a multi-step approach in resolving the performance profile. As per our initial set of queries we would evaluate the availability of a high-level software architecture specification. We would evaluate opportunities for improving performance utilization and bottlenecks in the application per the specifics of the architecture. We would evaluate the application deployment in a cloud environment and support for virtualization technology. This would allow for application portability on a host of platforms and ensure scalability.

We would evaluate the application throughput requirements in the end-to-end internet. This would include all memory and network bandwidth in the system that would be utilized in a finite amount of time. We would ensure that there is no saturation of resources on all the data pipes in the platform. Data intensive workloads are usually writing large amounts of data to and from memory including serving the information to a client on the network. Consequently, as per the application requirements we would evaluate the average and peak bandwidth requirements for all the interfaces on the platform. This would ensure a first order evaluation of the application requirements.

We would then evaluate the application in Linux perf De Melo [2010]. For the purposes of our performance profiling we will be using the Linux perf utility. Additionally, we would benchmark the application in the M5 simulator. Simulation gives us the ability to evaluate the application stack in a full system environment. We are able to view the function call trace and kernel system calls. Utilities like doxygen and gprof output a call graph for the source code statically at compile time enabling us to view function calls to locking / synchronization primitives. It outputs the control flow graph to view the structure of the program.

3.8 Rationale behind suggested solution

Perf supports performance modeling of a variety of events in the user application and kernel code. We are able to capture this data in the OS and output it to the customer in a web interface. The other set of utilities do not provide sufficient information profiling other than compute utilization and availability of memory resources. There is no capability to view thread resources in the system. Linux pthreads are scheduled and provisioned in the OS to enable performance scalability.

Utilities like gprof and doxygen support creation of UML and call graph. These enable visualization of the application function call and libraries used. They show percentage utilization of application code and opportunities for optimization.

3.9 Estimation

- Java KLOC per week = 0.85

- Python KLOC per week = 0.75

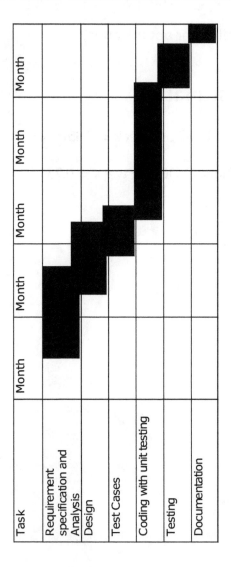

Task	Month	Month	Month	Month	Month
Requirement specification and Analysis	■				
Design		■			
Test Cases		■			
Coding with unit testing				■	
Testing					■
Documentation					■

Estimated Effort (PD)

Sl.	Modules	Estimated LOC	CUT	Requirement	Design	Architecture	Testing	Total
1	Compilation and library support	2000	12	3	4	1	9	29
2	Code annotation	1000	6	1	2	1	4	14
3	Simulator integration	1000	6	1	2	1	4	14
4	Operating System integration	2000	12	3	4	1	9	29

5	Virtualiz-ation	1500	9	2	3	1	7	22
6	Perform-ance analysis	2000	12	3	4	1	9	29
7	Input data to Elastic-search	1000	6	1	2	1	4	14
8	Kibana visualiza-tion	2000	12	3	4	1	9	29

Table 3.2: WBS

3.10   SDLC

3.10.1   SDLC model to be used

We use an Agile, continuous development SDLC model. Incremental development is used to deliver the product in short iterations of 1 to 4 weeks. Incremental delivery includes functions and features that have been developed. Continuous integration is used to integrate work frequently. Each integration is verified and tested in an automated build to detect errors. This enables the rapid development of cohesive software.

3.10.2   Rationale

Agile development and continuous integration. Enabled early detection and integration of defect and ensures code quality. Development happens in short iterations with fully automated regression tests. High level functional requirements are documented as user stories. Software development follows a model of Fig. 3.4.

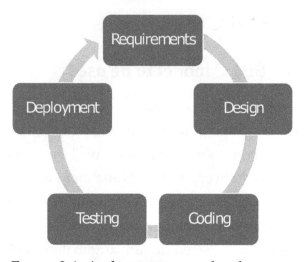

Figure 3.4: Agile continuous development

- Requirements – Design – Coding – Testing – Deployment

Agile focuses on individuals and interactions, working software, customer collaboration and responding to change. Quality is maintained through the use of automated unit testing, test driven development, design patterns and code refactoring.

3.10.3 Suggested Customizations proposed

We would use Lean techniques and Kanban. These ensure standardization and balance of the development environment.

3.11 Architectural (non-functional) requirements

- Interoperability

- Scalability

- Quality of Service

- Time, Cost and Productivity

- Distributed Complex Sourcing

- Faster Delivery of Innovation

- Increasing Complexity

- SaaS vs. PaaS

- Number of users, usage model

- Reuse of Web Services

- Agile, continuous development

- QOS is supported in tiered cloud service provider

3.12 Critical success factors

- Compatibility of development environments.

- Availability of source code and High-level architecture specification.

- Service Oriented Architecture (SOA)

- Linux based application hosted to run in a cloud platform.

Platforms while constantly updating themselves there is a standardization of functionality around the Linux open source movement. There has been a proliferation of development on the Linux platform and enabled commoditization of computing technology. Enterprises are now able to host a distributed platform at a marginal expense. Availability of open source software has accelerated the development of applications. Access to compiler technology in the GNU compiler collection has driven availability of shared libraries and the Linux file system. Applications can share run-time environments. Additionally, availability of version control systems has enabled collaboration across the conventional barriers.

We consequently choose an open source solution for our performance profiler. Availability of symbol tagged application libraries enables us to view runtime statistics including kernel system calls. Applications like top and perf provide system visibility in the Linux kernel. System performance information is captured using performance counters.

- Quality of service

- User base

- Open Source, Intellectual property, Revenue, Products and services

- Licensing, R&D, Open innovation, open source. Strategy vary in business needs

3.13 Architectural overview of the requirement and the feasibility in Linux operating system

Linux supports a host of virtualization and performance profiling tools Du et al. [2011]. A virtualized architecture consists of – Fig. 3.5.

1. Data collection

    (a) sysstat package – iostat, pidstat

    (b) sar, atop

2. Online data - top

    (a) iotop, iftop

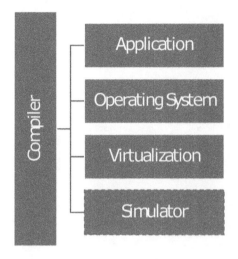

Figure 3.5: Host architecture

3. Tracing – strace, perf_events, mutrace

4. Application profiling. perf. gprof

5. Virtualization performance. VMware

6. Simulator. M5

The customer is interested in profiling the application on a host platform. Fig. 3.6 shows the characteristics of a host platform and n-tier application stack. As architects we are able to evaluate

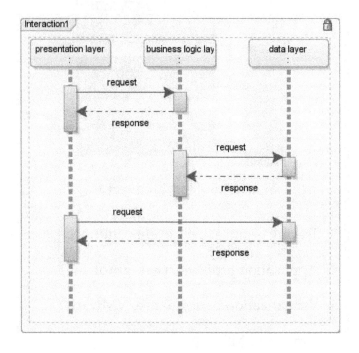

Figure 3.6: N-tier, SOA

the solution using the high-level specification. An architecture use case, sequence diagram would provide us with insight on the specific usage model. We are able to investigate bottlenecks in the application. Availability of performance profiling utilities enable us to evaluate the application latency profiling requirements.

3.13.1   Linux Perf

Perf is a performance profiling tool for Linux. It supports trace functionalities for various file system, block layer and syscall events. Tracepoints and instrumentation points are placed at logical locations in the application and kernel code. These have negligible overhead and are used by the perf command to collect information on timestamps and stack traces. It uses a set of performance counters to record and output a report for the application code.

3.13.2   Intel VTune

VTune is a proprietary performance profiling utility Malladi [2009]. It supports the implementation
of performance counters that are used to profile the
application. It supports a GUI and command line
interface. It is capable of monitoring thread level
and process level performance. It supports compute
performance, threading, scalability and bandwidth
monitoring - Fig. 3.7.

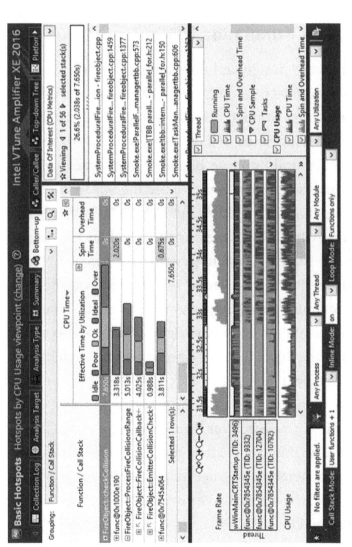

Figure 3.7: Intel VTune

3.13.3 Simulation M5

Simulator design and development explores a high-level architecture design space. Simulation enables the user to evaluate various deployment topologies are varying level of abstraction. It examines the architectural building blocks in the context of performance optimization. We use the M5 architectural simulator developed at the University of Michigan, Ann Arbor. It enables us to model an end-to-end client server simulation with the native OS and application stack. There is a minimal overhead in modeling the various system components. However, the flexibility in modeling performance coupled with the high level design knowledge enable for an efficient resolution of application performance constraints.

In our research on PicoServer Kgil et al. [2006], we were able to evaluate a generic architecture for the next generation internet based on internet protocols and open standards. We proposed an architecture for Web N with 10 billion users online.

We extend this research further in proposing a generic architectural framework for performance modeling. Given an architecture specification we are able to upfront evaluate dependency graphs and bottlenecks in the design. We take various approaches from compiler development in implementing efficient scheduling algorithms for scaling application in the cloud.

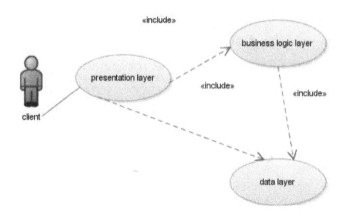

Figure 3.8: 3-tier use case diagram

Fig. 3.8 shows the architecture of an n-tier application in the cloud. Service Oriented Architecture

(SOA) applications consist of a discrete function unit that provides services to other components using a web-based protocol. A typical 3-tier application consists of a presentation layer which provides the user interface functionality. It accesses a business logic layer (middle layer) and data layer. The application is typically consolidated in a tiered cloud service provider in a SaaS, PaaS and IaaS model using a private, public cloud.

In Fig. 3.9, we demonstrate the functionality of a server in the cloud which consists of compute, memory and network. With the proliferation of the internet and globalization we are seeing a commoditization of the infrastructure layer. Increasingly the server components are available as pluggable building blocks that scale in the internet. We see that a server comprises of compute and network blocks that are used to access memory. Additionally, some architectures enable direct access to network elements to improve performance and reduce wait and synchronization times.

We evaluate the opportunities for building a set

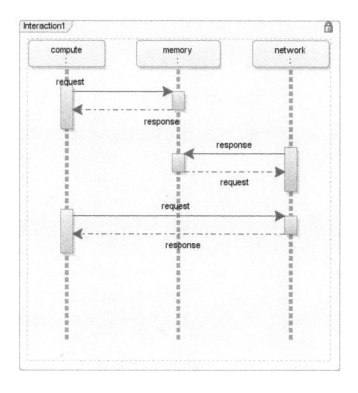

Figure 3.9: Web server

of heuristics for performance profiling including ad
hoc and statistical techniques and algorithms such
as shortest path, directed / un-directed graphs and

minimum spanning tree. Evaluate the dynamic call tree.

3.14 Types of process wait state used to achieve the profiling

Unix POSIX supports a variety of multi-threading and multi-process synchronization primitives. Pthread library is used to implement multi-threading. It supports the creation of threads using pthread_create and synchronization wait using pthread_join. Pthread supports the use of mutually exclusive locks through the use of pthread_mutex_t.

Unix supports multiprocessing capabilities through the use of fork, join. Multi-processor synchronization is implemented using wait and semaphore locks semget, semop. Additionally, there are a host of programming practices that help in the implementation of efficient parallel code with reduced wait times, starvation and deadlocks /

livelocks. Linux top enables viewing of various system statistics including user / kernel mode, idle and I/O wait. Perf supports the profiling of sleep and wait time in a program. These are obtained using the perf profiling events sched.

```
>> perf record -e sched:* -g -o perf.data.raw <<
   application>>
>> perf inject -v -s -i perf.data.raw -o perf.
   data


>> perf report --stdio --show-total-period -i
   perf.data
```

Latency is derived from multiple sources including scheduler, I/O and context switch. A waiting process can be blocked on events including availability of network, access to memory Ghemawat et al. [2003]. Multi-process systems enable optimization of the wait time by scheduling priority processes while a concurrent process is waiting on an external resource. There are various sources of latency in the Linux kernel

- Call to disk

- Memory management

- Fork and exit of a process

For an application blocked on I/O, we will see a latency on a read / write response to memory mapped input output (MMIO). Application driver code accesses a reserved section of the system memory map to communicate with external devices. Delayed access to a memory location results in an increased execution time of the driver library. MMIO's are implemented using kernel ioread and iowrite. Address information is configured using ioremap.

perf supports profile gathering for various types of events sched, cpu-clock, syscalls, ext4, block.

```
>> perf record -e sched:* -e cpu-clock -e
   syscalls:* -e ext4:* -e block:* <<application
   >>
```

We investigate the opportunities for reducing wait times in a multi-threaded, multi-process workload. We see that a large amount of time is used in sched events including pthread mutex and join - Fig. 3.10.

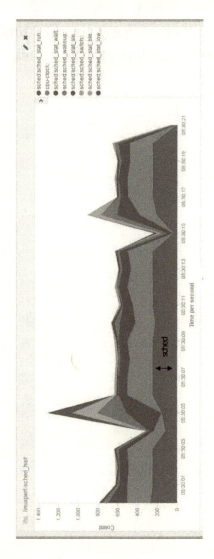

Figure 3.10: Multi-threaded/process use case

3.14.1   Xenoprof architecture

Xenoprof is an open source profiling utility base
on OProfile 3.11. It is developed on the Xen virtual
machine environment and enables the user to gather
system wide data. Xen is an open source virtual
machine monitor (VMM). OProfile can be used
to profile kernel and user level applications and
libraries. It enables profiling of applications running
in a virtualized environment.

Listing 3.1: xenoprof output

```
Function        %Instructions  Module
e1000_intr      13 .32 e1000
tcp_v4_rcv      8 .23   vmlinux
main    5 .47   rcv22
```

Virtualization profiling mechanisms provide real
time capabilities vs. a simulator. As all the application system calls are serviced in the virtualization en-
gine it is suitable to extend the VMM to support profiling. This functionality enables gathering of system
wide data.

High level architecture specification enables us to

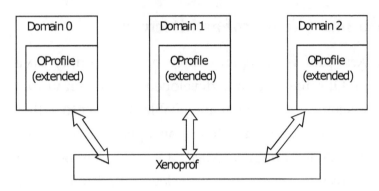

Figure 3.11: Xenoprof architecture

define a dependency graph for the application. This is facilitated by the availability of source code. A compiler is a sequential batch architecture - Fig. 3.12. AST represents the structure of the source code. Parser turns flat text into a tree. AST is a kind of a program intermediate form (IR).

Compilers and translators. Compilers translate information from one representation to another. Most commonly, the information is a program. Compilers translate from high-level source code to low-level code. Translators transform representations at the same level of abstraction.

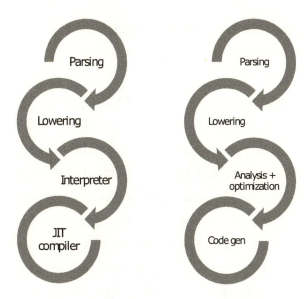

Figure 3.12: V8 JS, g++ compiler

- Windows – 50 million LOC

- Google internet services – 2 billion LOC

Compilers enables us to evaluate the application dependency graphs at compile time. It allows us to find cyclical dependencies in the program that might cause a deadlock. At runtime we would find extremely large idle wait time consumed by a blocking thread. In such scenarios the OS scheduler would stop the process and release its resources and restart.

A number of IDE's support the generation of a dependency graph for software profiling. MS Visual Studio generates a dependency for the Project Solution. A Dynamic call tree can be used to evaluate application critical paths at architecture design time.

Additionally, programs like strace output library information and can be used to evaluate program execution paths. strace provides system wide profiling including accesses to kernel system calls. Trace utilities like strace, ltrace and dtrace can be used to profile system performance.

```
>> strace -rT
<<strace output>>
```

3.15 Mechanism used to get the profiling data

3.15.1 Linux perf

Performance data metrics will be gathered using the perf utility. There are a large number of Unix programs that are available for performance profiling including top, iostat and sar. We run the perf utility in user mode to collect data for a specific application. The call-graph option is used to obtain function subtree information

```
>> perf record -g <<application>>
```

We can profile system wide metrics using perf sleep. This enables the perf utility to run in the background while the application is running on the host platform. This approach can be used in validating system state for network and web server applications like tomcat and apache web server. perf captures performance data for various shared libraries including system kernel drivers. Users can profile drivers loaded using insmod, lsmod.

```
/lib/modules/kernel/drivers/ .ko
/lib/ .so
```

```
>> perf record -a sleep <<N>> &
<<application>>
```

Recorded data is saved in a file perf.data for offline use. There a variety of utilities that enable viewing the data. We use the report implementation to view a percentage utilization of the shared libraries and functions in the application - Listing 3.2.

```
>> perf report
```

Listing 3.2: perf output

```
29.88%   a.out libstdc++.so.6.0.19 [.] std::
    basic_ostream<char, std::char_traits<char
    > >& std::__ostream_insert<char, std::
    char_traits<char>>(std::basic_ostream<
    char, std::char_traits<char> >&, char
    const*, long)
```

17.53%   a.out libstdc++.so.6.0.19 [.] std::
      basic_filebuf<char, std::char_traits<char
      > >::xsputn(char const*, long)

10.09%   a.out libstdc++.so.6.0.19 [.] std::
      basic_streambuf<char, std::char_traits<
      char> >::xsputn(char const*, long)

 7.60%   a.out libstdc++.so.6.0.19 [.] std::
      ostream::sentry::sentry(std::ostream&)

 5.86%   a.out libc-2.19.so   [.]
      __memcpy_sse2_unaligned

 5.50%   a.out libstdc++.so.6.0.19 [.] std::
      basic_ostream<char, std::char_traits<
      char> >& std::operator<< <std::
      char_traits<char>>(std::basic_ostream<
      char, std::char_traits<char> >&, char
      const*)

 4.67%   a.out [kernel.kallsyms] [k] 0
      xffffffff811ee670

 4.31%   a.out libc-2.19.so   [.] strlen

 3.05%   a.out libstdc++.so.6.0.19 [.] std::
      codecvt<char, char, __mbstate_t>::
      do_always_noconv() const

 2.26%   a.out a.out   [.]

```
           _ZStlsISt11char_traitsIcEERSt13basic_
           ostreamIcT_ES5_PKc@plt
1.66%   a.out libstdc++.so.6.0.19 [.]
           strlen@plt
1.66%   a.out libstdc++.so.6.0.19 [.]
           _ZSt16__ostream_insertIcSt11char_
           traitsIcEERSt13basic_
           ostreamIT_T0_ES6_PKS3_l@plt
1.54%   a.out libstdc++.so.6.0.19 [.]
           memcpy@plt
1.07%   a.out a.out              [.] foo()
0.99%   a.out libstdc++.so.6.0.19 [.]
           _ZNSo6sentryC1ERSo@plt
0.91%   a.out libstdc++.so.6.0.19 [.]
           _ZNSt15basic_streambufIcSt11char_
           traitsIcEE6xsputnEPKcl@plt
0.83%   a.out a.out              [.] main
0.55%   a.out a.out              [.] bar()
0.04%   a.out libstdc++.so.6.0.19 [.] std::
           __basic_file<char>::xsputn_2(char const
           *, long, char const*, long)
```

3.15.2 Network drivers

We evaluate the performance of the Linux network drivers using perf events sock, net and skb. scsi information is obtained using the scsi event.

```
>> perf record -e sock:* -e net:* -e skb:* -e
   scsi:* -e cpu-clock <<application>>
```

3.15.3 gprof

gprof is used to profile data using compiler annotated binary format. Application is compiled using the –pg option.

```
>> g++ -pg <<application.cpp>>
```

After the program has been compiled it will output a gmon.out file on run containing the application performance information. This can be viewed in the gprof application.

```
>> gprof <<application>>
```

Listing 3.3: gprof output

% time	cumulative seconds	self seconds	calls	self ms/call	total ms/call
41.64	0.12	0.12			

name

% time	cumulative seconds	self seconds	calls	self ms/call	total ms/call

main

41.64   0.12   0.12

    name

31.23   0.21   0.09   1   90.56   90.56

    foo()

26.02   0.29   0.08   1   75.47   166.02

    bar()

 0.00   0.29   0.00   3   0.00   0.00

        std::operator|(std::_Ios_Openmode, std::

        _Ios_Openmode)

 0.00   0.29   0.00   1   0.00   0.00

        _GLOBAL__sub_I__Z3foov

 0.00   0.29   0.00   1   0.00   0.00

        __static_initialization_and_destruction_0(

        int, int)

Simulators enables full-system visibility including application and OS. Simulation provides the user with a range of metrics related to application performance. Additionally, with the availability of simula-

tor and application OS source code, the user can customize debug messages to be outputted in the simulator and kernel dmesg logs. This enables us to evaluate the metrics in an offline mode and profile application characteristics including function bottlenecks.

Unix mutrace is used to obtain thread mutex debug information including contention and wait time -
Listing 3.4. It provides information on the number of
mutex locks used in the design, the number of times
the lock changed and the average wait time for each
lock.

Listing 3.4: mutrace output

```
Mutex #  Locked Changed   Cont. tot.Time[ms] avg
   .Time[ms] max.Time[ms] Flags
     0        8       4       4    45381.448
   .     5672.681   6303.132 M-.?-.
```

There are a host of utilities that enable measuring
network packet latency. Systemtap provides the user
with the ability to define event handlers for the Linux
kernel system calls. The user is able to log system
calls and event timing information.

111

A RETROSPECTIVE ON ENABLING A
CONNECTED WORLD

Availability of driver source code and build environment enables the user to add printk KERN_DEBUG messages in the kernel logs. These provide timing information for the driver execution. However, the driver libraries have to be rebuilt.

Compilers support the generation of an Abstract Syntax Tree (AST). This can be used to traverse multi-threaded, multi-process libraries to obtain critical path information. Availability of output from gprof and doxygen enables us to view the frequently used libraries and function calls. Compilers enable us to evaluate a static compile time profile for the application code. A control flow graph (CFG) is a graph representation of the user code. They are built recursively at compile time and are a high-level representation of the source code.

- CFG = (N, E)

- N – Set of nodes

- $E \subseteq N \times N$ – Set of edges

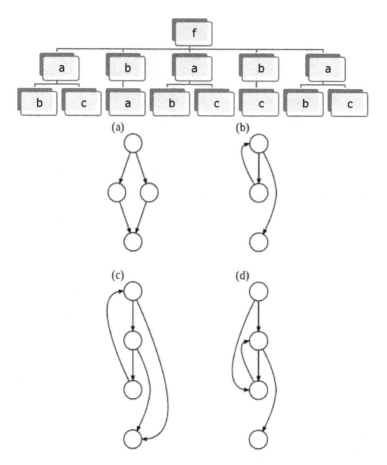

Figure 3.13: Control flow graph

Nodes in the graph constitute the basic blocks in application code including the function call and libraries accessed. These are used to evaluate critical paths in the design and dependency chains. Application profiling at compile time enables the user to profile the application during architecture design. The CFG is essential to compiler optimizations and static analysis. It is used in various directed approaches to latency reduction including scheduling and parallelism.

Compilers support a variety of optimizations including dead code elimination, common sub-expression elimination, loop invariant code motion, loop unrolling and parallelization. Detection of independent sub-graphs in the application code is used in application parallelizing. Function call and for loops can be partitioned by the compiler at compile time to optimize the application code for a multi-process / distributed cloud platform. Addition of user directives in the application code enables auto-partitioning of the code to ensure performance scalability.

3.16 Data storage, retrieval and presentation

We explore the usage of various visualization features in presenting the perf report data to the customer. We use the script command to output a raw report for the performance data. This includes information on the application command, time stamp and shared library related to the event. This data is exported into an Excel csv file.

Perf supports a set of command line utilities that can be used to visualize the report data information.

```
>> perf report --call-graph --stdio
```

Script is used to display and store a trace output for the test run.

```
>> perf script
```

3.16.1 Logstash

Logstash is used to input the user data into Kibana. A conf file is used to setup the Logstash pipeline –

Fig. 3.14.

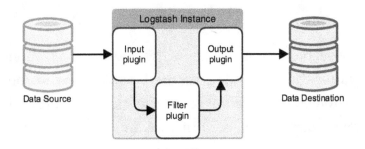

Figure 3.14: Logstash pipeline

We use the csv input filter to read the csv data file. An output filter is used to add the data to the Elasticsearch index. A template format is specified for reading the csv column values in the date time and string format. Time values of ss.SSS are used to read the perf event logs.

```
>> cat linuxperf.csv | logstash -f linuxperf.
   conf
```

3.16.2 Elasticsearch

Elasticsearch is a distributed and scalable data store. It provides search and analytics capabilities with Rest services. It supports indexing of a JSON document. Input is through Logstash.

3.16.3 Kibana

The data set is loaded in Kibana and a visualization dashboard is created to display the performance data to the customer.

- Data output in json format

- Stored in Kibana Elasticsearch

- Input using Logstash

```
>> curl 'localhost:9200/_cat/indices?v'
>> curl -XDELETE 'http://localhost:9200/
   linuxperf'
>> curl -XPUT localhost:9200/_bulk --data-binary
    @linuxperf.json
```

Availability of user data in a csv format enables us to store the data in a NoSQL database like MongoDB. Documents are stored in the database in the json format consisting of field value pairs. MongoDB provides high performance data persistence. A collection is created for the perf data. Data is then input to the database using the pymongo library. Users can insert, update documents in the database using json dictionary values.

Alternatively, the Linux perf data is stored in the run folder in the perf.data file. This is used alongside a host of perf report utilities to view the application call graph and utilization information.

gprof similary supports output in the gmon.out format. Applications are compiled in g++ for profiling using the symbol table information in the application binary. Run-time application call graph information is stored in the gmon.out file for profiling. gprof profiles function execution utilization information.

3.17 Characteristics of the user interface and the details about its functionality

Kibana is an open source framework for data visualization Gupta [2015]. It enables the user to analyze and explore structured and unstructured data in an intuitive interface. It supports the use of graphs, histogram and pie charts on large amounts of data. Users can view and discover the data in the UI. They can create various visualizations that can be integrated into a comprehensive dashboard. Fig. 3.15 shows a custom dashboard implemented for the Linux perf data.

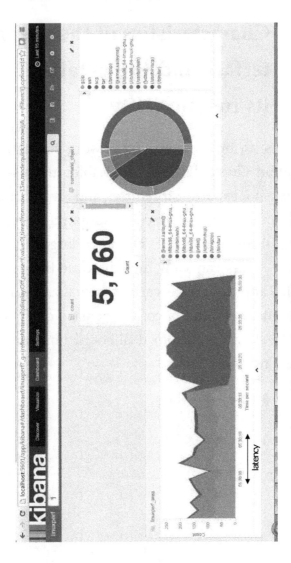

Figure 3.15: Kibana dashboard

3.17.1 Kibana user interface visualization

We evaluate a network workload consisting of a secure file transfer and zip compression of the data. As can be seen in the data a large amount of time is utilized in the libcrypto and gzip application. The histogram plots the total number of events per second as recorded / reported in perf. We additionally output a pie chart of the percentage of utilization for each application and the shared libraries accessed at runtime. We capture the data for all resources on the system for the duration of the application.

As the data is input in Kibana using Logstash, we create an index for the loaded data. The data can now be viewed as a list of input values for discovery. We use this data to create a set of visualizations. We create an area plot for the performance data using the logged time values in ss.SSS. We use the date histogram feature on the X-axis and split the plot using the run time command information. We create a pie chart using the command and corresponding shared library information in a sub-plot. Time series values are encoded in the date number format. Other input data is input in the string format with the option 'not_analyzed' set.

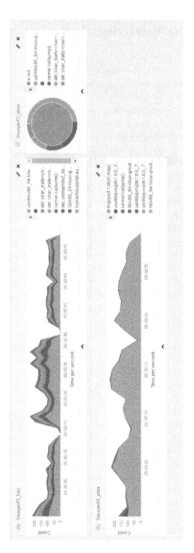

Figure 3.16: Kibana visualization

3.17.2   Python, MongoDB, Tomcat server

We additionally investigate the use of a NoSQL database in storing the results data. This is an architecture deployed in the Holmes Helpdesk platform. Python is used to update the performance profiling data in MongoDB code. This is then output to the customer in a HTML file in a DataTable - Fig. 3.17.

Show [10 v] entries
Search: [ ]

Overhead	Command	Shared Object	User Level	Symbol
28.15	firefox-bin	libxul.so	[usr]	0xd10b45
28.15	firefox-bin	libxul.so	[usr]	0xd10b45
4.45	swapper	[kernel.kallsyms]	[k]	mwait_idle_with_hints
4.45	swapper	[kernel.kallsyms]	[k]	mwait_idle_with_hints
4.26	swapper	[kernel.kallsyms]	[k]	read_hpet
4.26	swapper	[kernel.kallsyms]	[k]	read_hpet
2.13	firefox-bin	firefox-bin	[usr]	0x1e3d
2.13	firefox-bin	firefox-bin	[usr]	0x1e3d
1.40	unity-panel-ser	libglib-2.0.so.0.2800.6	[usr]	0x886f1
1.40	unity-panel-ser	libglib-2.0.so.0.2800.6	[usr]	0x886f1

Showing 1 to 10 of 10 entries

Previous 1 Next

Figure 3.17: HTML DataTable

HTML DataTable. JavaScript DataTables code runs natively on the HTML file allowing the user to browse, sort the performance data. A Tomcat server is enabled to output the MongoDB performance data to a Java Servlet so the customer can access the information remotely - Fig. 3.3.

3.18 Functional and nonfunctional requirements of the profiler

The performance profiler has been developed for a Linux platform and supports the Unix POSIX function calls. It should support the C++, Java development libraries and run-time environments. There should be a compatible JRE running on the system. Additionally, a lot of the UI features will be supported in a browser based application. The platform features like Kibana and DataTables will use a browser.

- The application must support the linux-common-tools corresponding to the kernel release.

- Availability of High-level architecture documents.

- Requirements engineering – Implementation – Testing – Evaluation

We will be exploring the design space of a Linux performance profiler that would allow us to evaluate bottlenecks arising from an inefficiently designed application. The application would support an intuitive user interface and present a metrics dashboard to the user highlighting the compute utilization for the application code. The user would be able to view the total run time for the application and library wise break down of run-time utilization. We would design the user interface such that any user would be able to evaluate the performance characteristics of an application.

The profiler would run in a Linux based environment enabling the reuse of existing Unix kernel and application libraries. There are a number of Unix utilities that support application and system level performance monitoring. For the purposes of our investigation we will explore a hybrid of open source and COTS implementation including a simulator and compiler design. Design of the simulator and compiler are highly intensive projects with simulator designs running into 100K+ LOC and compilers at 50K+ LOC. As we will be exploring open source alternatives in our design. We will look at the use of the M5 simulator which is a full-system architectural simulator and the Unix g++ and java compilers.

Unix standards enable us to run a host of application on a shared platform architecture. Additionally, with the availability of open libraries and kernel binaries the user is able to observe the performance of an application in the Linux environment. Utilities like top and iostat enable us to view system compute utilization and I/O wait times. We will assume the functionality of an SOA application running on a

web-based platform. The application would run on
the OS natively enabling us to benchmark the application and gather data for offline viewing. We would
provide all the application utilities on the test platform. The user would launch the application using
a script which would gather the data and input it to
Kibana using Logstash. We would run Kibana and
Elasticsearch on a user machine for viewing the results data. It is possible that running the data viewer
utility on the same test platform could corrupt the
data. Alternatively, we could run the Kibana UI on a
VMM on the same physical machine.

- Non-functional requirements include data
  requirements, constraints and quality requirements.

- Product requirements – portability, reliability,
  usability, efficiency, performance

- Organization – delivery, implementation, standards

- Availability of documented code.

Eclipse is an open source IDE and supports a variety of programming languages including plugin functionality. Eclipse supports the standard GNU environment for compiling, building and debugging applications. The CDT is a plugin which enables development of C/C++ applications in Eclipse. It enables functionality including code browsing, syntax highlighting and code completion.

Eclipse supports a number of programming languages including C/C++, Java, PHP, XML, and HTML. It is an open source IDE and can be used on multiple platforms including Windows, Linux. It supports plugins to extend the functionality of the IDE for source code language modeling and analysis.

Figure 3.18: Stages of compilation parser

We use the CDT to function as a compiler frontend - Fig. 3.18. The CDT uses a translation unit to represent a source file cpp and h. The CDT core supports a Visitor API which is used to traverse the AST. AST rewrite API is used to update the source code. We access the code AST using the Eclipse CDT API.

We evaluate the generation of a dependency graph for software profiling. The AST is used to profile critical application paths including access to lock and synchronization primitives. These enable us to evaluate a latency profile at design time. Eclipse supports a plugin to analyze library dependencies. MS Visual Studio generates a dependency graph for all the drivers and files in the solution architecture.

3.19 Summary

We have looked at architectures for the next generation enterprise including end to end solutions for the web infrastructure. These highlight the challenges in bringing billions of users online on a commodity platform. There is a large opportunity in enabling technology consumption for more than a billion users. Technologies like social media, enterprise mobility, data analytics and cloud are disrupting the enterprise. Research and Development (R&D) is an enabler for the enterprise. We are in the midst of a modern day information revolution enabled by increased availability of technology. I have highlighted the technology direction and challenges that we as architects foresee and resolve. These include researching machine learning, compilers, algorithms and developing efficient language models to enable applications and systems in the enterprise.

Without a robust termination you could get stuck in a loop #fibonacci #recursion #goldenratio

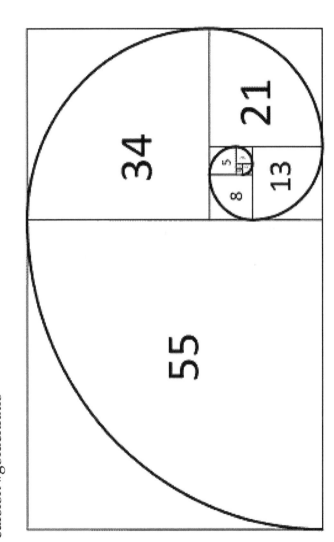

A RETROSPECTIVE ON ENABLING A CONNECTED WORLD

Chapter 4

Eclipse CDT code analysis and unit testing

In this chapter we look at the Eclipse IDE and its support for CDT (C/C++ Development Tools). Eclipse is an open source IDE and supports a variety of programming languages including plugin functionality. Eclipse supports the standard GNU environment for compiling, building and debugging applications. The CDT is a plugin which enables development of C/C++ applications in eclipse. It enables functionality including code browsing, syntax highlighting and code completion. We verify a 50X improvement in LOC automation for Fake class .cpp / .h and class test .cpp code generation.

4.1   Introduction

Eclipse supports a number of programming languages including C/C++ Stroustrup [2013], web [c], Java, PHP, XML, and HTML. It is an open source IDE and can be used on multiple platforms including Windows, Linux. It supports plugins to extend the functionality of the IDE for source code language modeling and analysis.

In our paper we study the use of Eclipse to enable an automation framework for generation of unit tests and fake classes for code debug Hamill [2004]. Eclipse supports the parsing and compilation of code into an index file. The index file is used to store code binding information including identifiers bindings, source file location, macros and include files.

4.2 Stages of compilation parser

Source code
Lexical analysis
Syntax analysis
Semantic analysis

Token stream
Abstract Syntax Tree

Table 4.1: Stages of compilation parser

Scanning converts the input character stream into a stream of tokens. Eg. 'I' 'n' 't' is converted to a token object of type int. Preprocessing involves macro expansion, conditional compilation and inclusion of header files. Parsing converts the C++ language semantics into an abstract syntax tree structure web [d]. The AST is an intermediate program representation for the code and captures all the semantic information for the source - Table 4.2. Source code is optimized for human readability.

4.2.1 Lexical analysis

Natural language: "I shot an elephant in my pajamas"

I	shot	an	elephant	in	my	pajamas

Programming language: "if (a == 0) a = b + 1"

if	(	a	==	0	)	a	=	b	+	1

4.2.2 Syntax analysis

Natural Language

The	cat	sat	on	the	mat
det	noun	verb	prep	det	noun
subject		predicate	prep	object	

Programming language

if (a == 0)	a = b + 1
test	assignment
if-statement	

4.2.3 Semantic analysis

Natural Language

The	green	*apple*	ate	a	juicy	bug
det	adj	noun	noun	det	noun	noun

Programming language

if (a == 0)	a = *foo*
test	assignment

Semantic analysis will report an error.

4.3   CDT Core

We use the CDT to function as a compiler frontend
and use the AST to generate unit tests Dickheiser
[2006]. The CDT uses a translation unit to represent
a source file cpp and h. The CDT core supports a
Visitor API which is used to traverse the AST web
[b]. AST rewrite API is used to update the source
code. We access the code AST using the Eclipse CDT
API.

C-Model: ITranslationUnit for a workspace file

```
IPath path= new Path("project/folder/file.cpp");
IFile file= ResourcesPlugin.getWorkspace().
   getRoot().getFile(path);
```

139

```
// Create translation unit for file
ITranslationUnit tu= (ITranslationUnit)
    CoreModel.getDefault().create(file);
```

C-Model: ITranslationUnit for file in the editor

```
IEditorPart e= PlatformUI.getWorkbench().
    getActiveWorkbenchWindow().getActivePage().
    getActiveEditor();
// Access translation unit of the editor.
ITranslationUnit tu= (ITranslationUnit)
    CDTUITools.getEditorInputCElement(editor.
    getEditorInput());
```

C-Index: IIndex for project

```
ICProject project= CoreModel.getDefault().
    getCModel().getCProject("project");
IIndex index= CCorePlugin.getIndexManager().
    getIndex(project);
```

Eclipse supports the use of IBinding Gosling et al. [2014]. Binding completely represents the C/C++ entity. It contains information about the type of a variable, return type and parameters of a function. A compiler is used to translate one program representation to another. Most commonly the information is a program. We use the Eclipse CDT in our investigation to process the source tree and generate a set of Fake class and unit test files Li et al. [2011].

The CDT is not a compiler and is designed to support compiler frontend features. It is designed for performance and is able to parse code skipping included header files. The parsers do not perform any semantic analysis or type checking during the parse. The phases of parsing include scanning and preprocessing. During the scanning phase a stream of character inputs is converted into a stream of tokens. Preprocessing also involves macro expansion, conditional compilation and inclusion of header files. Parsing is used to convert the input token stream to an AST. The parser converts concrete syntax into an abstract syntax tree representation. The AST is used in semantic analysis of the code to implement type checking of the code definitions.

We implemented an ASTVisitorImpl class to traverse the code AST. This allows us to obtain all the declaration information for the functions in a class.

We traverse all declarations in the code. Function and constructor information is used to construct the Fake Class .cpp and .h header files. This is then integrated into the unit testing framework. We store a list of function declarations and class information to create the Fake class files and unit tests.

4.4   Fake class plugin UML

Figure 4.1: Fake class plugin UML

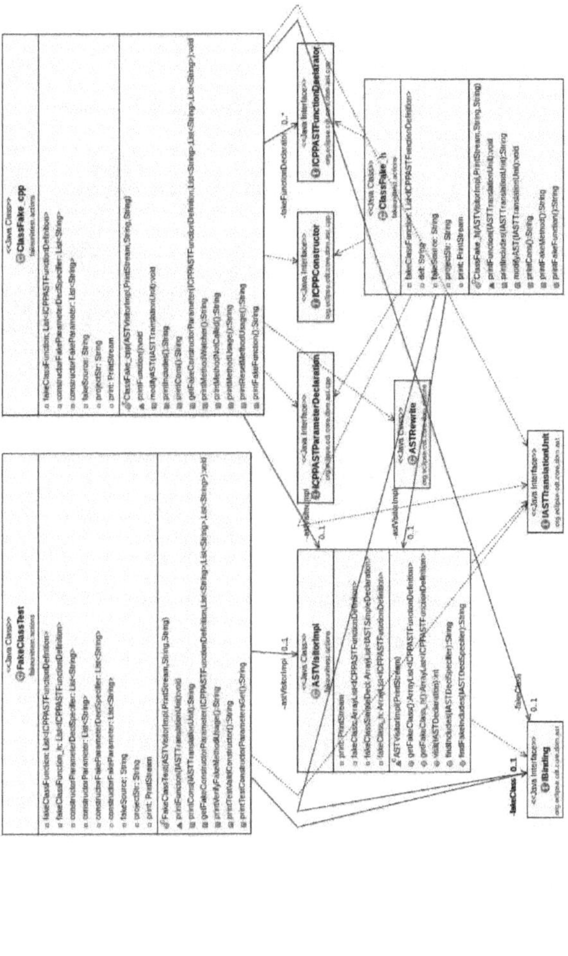

```
discovery/storage/
    FakeStorageSCSI_DiscoveryAlgorithm.cpp


FakeStorageSCSI_DiscoveryAlgorithm::
    FakeStorageSCSI_DiscoveryAlgorithm()
: StorageSCSI_DiscoveryAlgorithm()
, fake_run( "FakeStorageSCSI_DiscoveryAlgorithm
    ::run" )
, fake_associate( "
    FakeStorageSCSI_DiscoveryAlgorithm::associate
    " )
, fake_getDuplicatedHardDriveList( "
    FakeStorageSCSI_DiscoveryAlgorithm::
    getDuplicatedHardDriveList" )
, fake_addUniqueHardDrive( "
    FakeStorageSCSI_DiscoveryAlgorithm::
    addUniqueHardDrive" )
, fake_isDuplicateBackplane( "
    FakeStorageSCSI_DiscoveryAlgorithm::
    isDuplicateBackplane" )
}


void FakeStorageSCSI_DiscoveryAlgorithm::
```

```
    verifyFakeMethodUsage( const std::string&
    testCondition )
{
  TestUtility::verifyFakeMethodUsage( fake_run,
      testCondition );
  TestUtility::verifyFakeMethodUsage(
      fake_associate, testCondition );
  TestUtility::verifyFakeMethodUsage(
      fake_getDuplicatedHardDriveList,
      testCondition );
  TestUtility::verifyFakeMethodUsage(
      fake_addUniqueHardDrive, testCondition );
  TestUtility::verifyFakeMethodUsage(
      fake_isDuplicateBackplane, testCondition );
}


void FakeStorageSCSI_DiscoveryAlgorithm::run(
    UI_Facade& uiFacade )
{
  return fake_run( uiFacade );
}


discovery/storage/
```

145

```
StorageSCSI_DiscoveryAlgorithmTest.cpp
```

```
StorageSCSI_DiscoveryAlgorithm_data()
: fakeDeviceReporter()
, fakeDiscoveryRepository()
, fakeIoConnectionOperations()
, fakeTransportFactory()
, fakeDiscoveryOperationsFactory()
, fakeDiscoveredDeviceOperationsFactory()
, fakeFusionIO_AcceleratorFactory()
, fakePciOperationsFactoryPtr( new
    FakePCI_OperationsFactory() )
, fakeFileSystemOperations()
, fakeSmbiosOperationsPtr( new
    FakeSMBIOS_Operations() )
, fakeIloOperationsPtr( new iLO::
    Fake_iLO_Operations() )
, fakeTimeOperationsPtr( new FakeTimeOperations
    () )
, failureEventStatus( FakeEvt::failure )
, goodEventStatus()
{
}
```

Refactoring is changing restructuring existing code without changing its behaviour. We use the ASTRewrite class functionality to modify code dynamically by describing changes to the AST. Eclipse supports modification of specific code declarations in the source using the CDT.

```
IASTTranslationUnit tu = ...;
ASTRewrite r = ASTRewrite.create( tu );
IASTNode lit = r.createLiteralNode( String code
    );
r.replace( declaration, lit, null );
Change c = r.rewriteAST();
c.perform( new NullProgressMonitor() );
```

New AST nodes can be created using the getASTNodeFactory().

```
IASTBreakStatement breakStatement = tu.
    getASTNodeFactory().newBreakStatement();
```

However for our implementation in Fake class and unit test generation we use ASTRewrite createLiteralNode method. We however look at the use of getASTNodeFactory in implementing refac-

Parsing	Parsing
Lowering	Lowering
Interpreter	Analysis + Optimization
JIT compiler	Code gen

Table 4.2: V8 JS, g++ compiler

toring and extending the fake class and unit test functionality.

ASTRerwite uses the following functions to implement code refactoring.

```
void remove( IASTNode n, TextEditGroup eg )
ASTRewrite replace( IASTNode n, IASTNode repl,
    TextEditGroup eg )
ASTRewrite insertBefore( IASTNode p, IASTNode
    insPoint, IASTNode newN, TextEditGroup eg )
```

4.5 Summary

We enable an Eclipse CDT framework as a design for performance best practise. The developed unit test productivity accelerator, framework components facilitate source code integration. The plugin is developed for generation of unit test code and software engineering. Source files are input to the plugin in the project. We verify a 50X improvement in LOC automation for Fake class .cpp / .h and class test .cpp code. The open source plugin automates code analysis and unit test generation.

Chaos in the datacenter

Chapter 5

Cognitive Architecture for a Connected World

We propose a unified architecture for next generation cognitive, low cost, mobile internet. The end
user platform is able to scale as per the application
and network requirements. It takes computing out
of the data center and into end user platform. Internet enables open standards, accessible computing
and applications programmability on a commodity
platform. The architecture is a super-set to present

day infrastructure web computing. The Java virtual machine (JVM) derives from the stack architecture. Applications can be developed and deployed on a multitude of host platforms. $O(1) \leftrightarrow O(N)$. Computing and the internet today are more accessible and available to the larger community. Machine learning has made extensive advances with the availability of modern computing. It is used widely in NLP, Computer Vision, Deep learning and AI. A prototype device for mobile could contain N compute and N MB of memory.

5.1   Introduction

Application performance was a primary determinant of system performance. Processor and Memory technology determine system performance Kgil et al. [2006]. With the advent of the Internet, computing performance is increasingly being utilized in the network. Applications are internet based and network connectivity is central to the platform.

Network performance is a primary determinant of system. Existing internet connectivity are limited by technology capabilities Wi-Fi, 4G (Mbps).

Figure 5.1: Conventional computer platform components

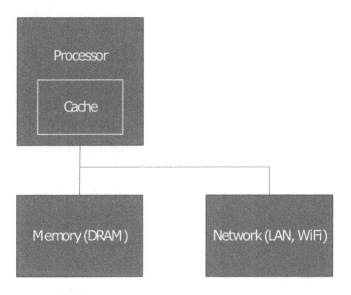

Conventional Computer platform components

- Processor, Cache

- Memory (DRAM)

- Network (LAN, Wi-Fi)

5.2 Industry Landscape & Market Challenges

Increasingly applications are internet based. Network performance is a primary determinant of system performance. Conventional computer was an in the box solution for desktop applications. The architecture was developed for high performance desktop applications. Processor, cache (GHz) coupled to high capacity Memory (DRAM). Fig. 5.1 shows a conventional platform with Processor and cache coupled to Memory and Network.

Processor technology speeds are increasing faster than DRAM memory technology. Processors are designed to operate at a high frequency >2 Ghz. Caches are coupled to the processor to facilitate execution at high speed. DRAM memory technology is designed for high density >2 GB. As a result, the platform is not able to scale to meet the network performance and system performance requirements.

Figure 5.2: Processor coupled to memory and network

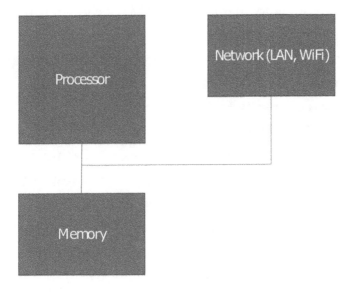

Network applications rely of moving data from network to memory and the processor - Fig. 5.2. As a result, system performance is determined by bandwidth throughput in the memory. Internet applications are consuming increasing bandwidth and will use $>1 - 10$ Gbps bandwidth in a mobile platform.

5.3 Technological and Operational challenges

Processor and memory (DRAM) technology have evolved independently to increase system performance. Processors were designed to run at high speeds (>2 GHz). Memory (DRAM) was designed for large capacity (>2 GB)

Until recently it was not feasible to integrate multi-Mb memory in a processor. Caches were used in the processor with application residing in main memory DRAM. However, with technological advances it is now possible to integrate multi-Mb memory (SRAM) in a processor. This enables us to re-evaluate the system hierarchy with processor, memory and network - Fig. 5.4.

Integrating large memory in the processor allows us to eliminate caches in the design. Desktop applications were constrained by technology performance Lindholm et al. [2014]. However recently we are seeing a saturation in application performance requirements. The Internet is today the platform for application enabling and the internet operational enablement is a driver of technology growth Berners-Lee [1989].

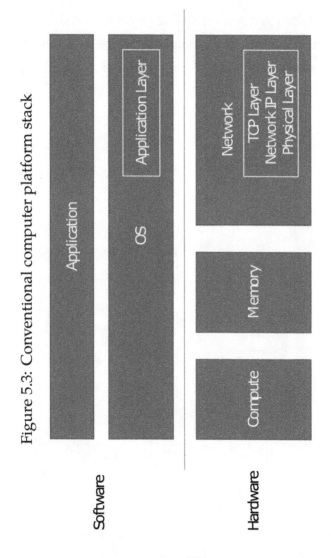

Figure 5.3: Conventional computer platform stack

CHAPTER 5. COGNITIVE ARCHITECTURE FOR A CONNECTED WORLD

We propose an architecture for the next generation enterprise including an end to end solution for the web infrastructure. This highlights the challenges in bringing billions of users online on a commodity platform. There is a large opportunity in enabling technology consumption for more than a billion users.

A conventional computer platform consists of - Fig. 5.3

Hardware:

- Processor and cache

- Memory (DRAM)

- Network TCP layer, IP layer, Physical layer – LAN, Wi-Fi, WiMAX, 5G, 4G

Software:

- Application

- OS Network Stack - Application layer

Figure 5.4: Proposed computer platform with compute (RISC, CISC) coupled to memory, no caches

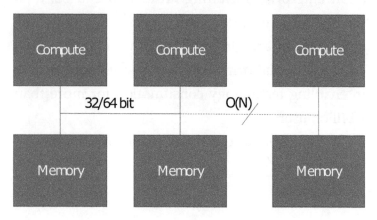

5.4 Proposed Solution

The architecture addresses technology challenges in scaling the next generation internet including efficiency in the data center Corbet et al. [2005]. The architecture enables high performance commodity computing in the end user platform enabling technology of scale. Machine learning libraries like TensorFlow Abadi et al. [2016] can be programmed on a homogeneous architecture fabric.

CHAPTER 5. COGNITIVE ARCHITECTURE FOR A CONNECTED WORLD

This facilitates an abstraction for the development of algorithms Abadi et al. [2015] and software on an open platform using a host of programming languages Hejlsberg et al. [2010].

Conventional computing platforms:

- Processor >2GHz

- Memory >2GB

Proposed architecture:

- Network Bandwidth 1 - 10 Gbps

As a metric, it is key to replicate scale the infrastructure maintaining redundancy to ensure quality of service in the end-to-end internet. These include Master-slave and P2P models.

The Stack machine[1] is a fundamental compute primitive. Processor and memory technology are now capable of integrating multi-Ghz and multi-Mb designs. There is a diminishing improvement for

---

[1]http://en.wikipedia.org/wiki/Stack_machine

Figure 5.5: Proposed platform with stack machine tightly coupled to memory, no caches

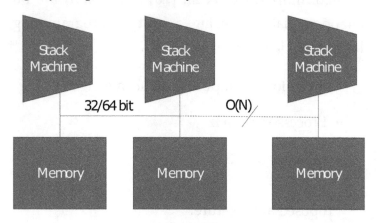

multi-Ghz processor designs as application memory is accessible in memory (DRAM).

Proposed architecture:

- Multiprocessor and SRAM memory tightly coupled – no caches

- Generic configurable Network I/O – LAN, Wi-Fi, WiMAX, 5G, 4G

- Programmable Network I/O - Network layers integrated in OS stack

5.5 Business Impact

We propose a high-performance general-purpose web computing platform using a tightly coupled processor (no caches L1, L2) and memory (SRAM) - Fig. 5.5. A shared memory CMP architecture allows for a turn key, low cost solution to mobile connectivity allowing tight integration of processor technology and application specific software stack. A prototype device for mobile could contain 4 compute and N MB of SRAM memory. $O(1) \leftrightarrow O(N)$.

As the device becomes accessible to more markets we would see increasing accessibility to the internet web [a]. Internet accessibility in a low-cost device enables scale in markets and applications. The platform uses general purpose processors in a shared memory environment to enable better programmability. Internet platforms enable open standards for technology development.

We are seeing a broader industry wide convergence and disruption. The idea is an absolutely vital cog in the technology stack.

- Modus ponens, Conjecture

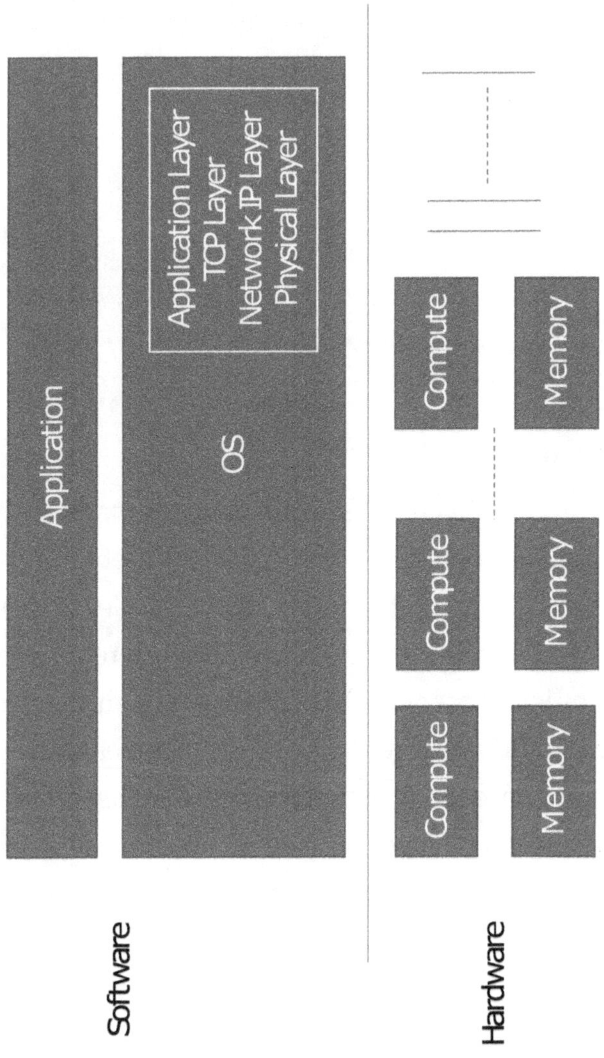

Figure 5.6: Proposed architecture stack

Figure 5.7: Systemic mixer fair

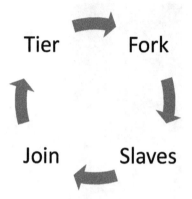

The architecture is a unified approach to bring next generation cognitive, low cost, mobile internet. The end user platform is able to scale as per the application requirements and network requirements in a efficient manner to improve cost, time to market, energy and accessibility - Fig. 5.6. It takes computing out of the data center and into end user platform enabling an internet of scale for the next century. Internet enables open standards, accessible computing and applications programmability on a commodity platform.

- Collaboration

- Finite in an infinite

- Industry matrix - Fig.5.7

- Ubiquitous

5.6 Summary

Increasing number of devices are being connected to the internet. The internet is an open platform for next generation technologies Faulkner et al. [2017]. Open platforms enable better collaboration and innovation. The future of the internet is mobile as >1 billion devices go online on IP. The presented architecture is a CMP design based on commodity processor and memory technology. We have an architecture with N (10's - 100's) compute connected to multi-MB SRAM memory using a shared memory system bus architecture. Number of compute and memory can scale in the power and performance requirements of the platform and the technology generation.

Schrödinger's cat. Did I hear a meow …

Bibliography

Android developer guide. http://developer.android.com/guide/index.html, a.

Api for c/c++ ast. http://help.eclipse.org/luna/index.jsp?topic=%2Forg.eclipse.cdt.doc.isv%2Fguide%2Fdom%2Findex.html, b.

Gnu g++. http://gcc.gnu.org, c.

Overview of parsing. http://wiki.eclipse.org/CDT/designs/Overview_of_Parsing, d.

M. Abadi, A. Agarwal, P. Barham, E. Brevdo, Z. Chen, C. Citro, G. S. Corrado, A. Davis, J. Dean, M. Devin, S. Ghemawat, I. Goodfellow,

A. Harp, G. Irving, M. Isard, Y. Jia, R. Jozefow-
icz, L. Kaiser, M. Kudlur, J. Levenberg, D. Mané,
R. Monga, S. Moore, D. Murray, C. Olah, M. Schus-
ter, J. Shlens, B. Steiner, I. Sutskever, K. Talwar,
P. Tucker, V. Vanhoucke, V. Vasudevan, F. Viégas,
O. Vinyals, P. Warden, M. Wattenberg, M. Wicke,
Y. Yu, and X. Zheng. TensorFlow: Large-scale
machine learning on heterogeneous systems, 2015.
URL https://www.tensorflow.org/. Software
available from tensorflow.org.

M. Abadi, P. Barham, J. Chen, Z. Chen, A. Davis,
J. Dean, M. Devin, S. Ghemawat, G. Irving, M. Isard, et al. Tensorflow: a system for large-scale machine learning. In *OSDI*, volume 16, pages 265–283,
2016.

M. Allamanis and C. Sutton. Mining source code
repositories at massive scale using language modeling. In *Proceedings of the 10th Working Conference on Mining Software Repositories*, pages 207–216.
IEEE Press, 2013.

S. Auer, C. Bizer, G. Kobilarov, J. Lehmann, R. Cyga-
niak, and Z. Ives. Dbpedia: A nucleus for a web
of open data» de the semantic web, busan. *Korea,
Springer*, 2007.

T. J. Berners-Lee. Information management: A pro-
posal. Technical report, 1989.

N. Binkert, B. Beckmann, G. Black, S. K. Reinhardt,
A. Saidi, A. Basu, J. Hestness, D. R. Hower, T. Kr-
ishna, S. Sardashti, et al. The gem5 simulator. *ACM
SIGARCH Computer Architecture News*, 39(2):1–7,
2011.

X. Carreras and L. Màrquez. Introduction to the
conll-2005 shared task: Semantic role labeling. In
*Proceedings of the ninth conference on computational
natural language learning*, pages 152–164. Association for Computational Linguistics, 2005.

J. Corbet, A. Rubini, and G. Kroah-Hartman. *Linux
Device Drivers, 3rd Edition*. O'Reilly Media, Inc.,
2005. ISBN 0596005903.

A. C. De Melo. The new linux'perf'tools. In *Slides from Linux Kongress*, volume 18, 2010.

J. Dean and S. Ghemawat. Mapreduce: simplified data processing on large clusters. *Communications of the ACM*, 51(1):107–113, 2008.

L. Del Corro and R. Gemulla. Clausie: clause-based open information extraction. In *Proceedings of the 22nd international conference on World Wide Web*, pages 355–366. ACM, 2013.

M. Dickheiser. *Game Programming Gems 6*, chapter 1. GAME DEVELOPMENT SERIES. Charles River Media, 2006. ISBN 9781584504504. URL `https://books.google.co.in/books?id=1PZQAAAAMAAJ`.

S. C. D'souza. System and method for extracting information from unstructured text, June 19 2018. US Patent App. 15/474,194.

J. Du, N. Sehrawat, and W. Zwaenepoel. Performance profiling of virtual machines. *Acm Sigplan Notices*, 46(7):3–14, 2011.

O. Etzioni, A. Fader, J. Christensen, S. Soderland, and M. Mausam. Open information extraction: The second generation. In *IJCAI*, volume 11, pages 3–10, 2011.

S. Faulkner, S. Moon, T. Leithead, A. Eicholz, and A. Danilo. HTML 5.2. W3C recommendation, W3C, Dec. 2017. https://www.w3.org/TR/2017/REC-html52-20171214/.

S. Ghemawat, H. Gobioff, and S.-T. Leung. *The Google file system*, volume 37. ACM, 2003.

J. Gosling, B. Joy, G. Steele, G. Bracha, and A. Buckley. *The Java Language Specification, Java SE 8 Edition*. Java Series. Pearson Education, 2014. ISBN 9780133900798. URL https://books.google.co.in/books?id=1DaDAwAAQBAJ.

Y. Gupta. *Kibana Essentials*. Packt Publishing Ltd, 2015.

P. Hamill. *Unit Test Frameworks*. O'Reilly, first edition, 2004. ISBN 0596006896.

A. Hejlsberg, M. Torgersen, S. Wiltamuth, and P. Golde. *C# Programming Language*. Addison-Wesley Professional, 4th edition, 2010. ISBN 0321741765, 9780321741769.

M. Honnibal and M. Johnson. An improved non-monotonic transition system for dependency parsing. In *Proceedings of the 2015 Conference on Empirical Methods in Natural Language Processing*, pages 1373–1378, Lisbon, Portugal, September 2015. Association for Computational Linguistics. URL https://aclweb.org/anthology/D/D15/D15-1162.

J. E. Hopcroft, R. Motwani, and J. D. Ullman. Introduction to automata theory, languages, and computation. *Acm Sigact News*, 32(1):60–65, 2001.

T. Kgil, S. D'Souza, A. Saidi, N. Binkert, R. Dreslinski, T. Mudge, S. Reinhardt, and K. Flautner.

Picoserver: Using 3d stacking technology to enable a compact energy efficient chip multiprocessor. In *Proceedings of the 12th International Conference on Architectural Support for Programming Languages and Operating Systems*, ASPLOS XII, pages 117–128, New York, NY, USA, 2006. ACM. ISBN 1-59593-451-0. doi: 10.1145/1168857.1168873. URL http://doi.acm.org/10.1145/1168857.1168873.

G. Li, I. Ghosh, and S. P. Rajan. Klover: A symbolic execution and automatic test generation tool for c++ programs. In *International Conference on Computer Aided Verification*, pages 609–615. Springer, 2011.

Y. Lin, J.-B. Michel, E. L. Aiden, J. Orwant, W. Brockman, and S. Petrov. Syntactic annotations for the google books ngram corpus. In *Proceedings of the ACL 2012 system demonstrations*, pages 169–174. Association for Computational Linguistics, 2012.

T. Lindholm, F. Yellin, G. Bracha, and A. Buckley. *The Java Virtual Machine Specification, Java SE 8 Edi-*

tion. Addison-Wesley Professional, 1st edition, 2014. ISBN 013390590X, 9780133905908.

Z. Mahmood and S. Saeed. *Software engineering frameworks for the cloud computing paradigm.* Springer, 2013.

R. K. Malladi. Using intel® vtune™ performance analyzer events/ratios & optimizing applications. *http://software.intel.com*, 2009.

D. Metzler and O. Kurland. Experimental methods for information retrieval. In *Proceedings of the 35th international ACM SIGIR conference on Research and development in information retrieval*, pages 1185–1186. ACM, 2012.

J.-B. Michel, Y. K. Shen, A. P. Aiden, A. Veres, M. K. Gray, J. P. Pickett, D. Hoiberg, D. Clancy, P. Norvig, J. Orwant, et al. Quantitative analysis of culture using millions of digitized books. *science*, page 1199644, 2010.

T. Mikolov, I. Sutskever, K. Chen, G. S. Corrado, and

J. Dean. Distributed representations of words and phrases and their compositionality. In *Advances in neural information processing systems*, pages 3111–3119, 2013.

A. OpenNLP. Apache software foundation. *URL http://opennlp.apache.org*, 2011.

R. Rastogi. Building knowledge bases from the web. In *Proceedings of the 18th International Conference on Management of Data*, pages 5–5. Computer Society of India, 2012.

D. Rohde. Tgrep2. Technical report, Technical report, Carnegie Mellon University. http://tedlab.mit.edu/ dr/Tgrep2, 2001.

B. Stroustrup. *The C++ programming language*. Pearson Education, 2013.
Images source: Twitter

Shaun D'Souza

About the Author

Shaun D'Souza has over 12 years experience in AI, ML, Software Engineering, R&D, Business. He has a varied experience in Computer Science and Engineering. Shaun completed his BS from Cornell University with a Double Major in Computer Science, Electrical and Computer Engineering, Cum Laude Honors in 2003. He completed his MSE in Electrical Engineering from the University of Michigan, Ann Arbor, Electrical Engineering and Computer Science Department in 2005. Shaun has worked in Software/Business researching machine learning, compilers, algorithms and systems. He has published papers and been granted a patent.